The Learning Mentor Manual

Stephanie George

Los Angeles | London | New Delhi
Singapore | Washington DC

SAGE Publications Ltd
1 Oliver's Yard
55 City Road
London EC1Y 1SP

SAGE Publications Inc.
2455 Teller Road
Thousand Oaks, California 91320

SAGE Publications India Pvt Ltd
B 1/I 1 Mohan Cooperative Industrial Area
Mathura Road
New Delhi 110 044

SAGE Publications Asia-Pacific Pte Ltd
33 Pekin Street #02-01
Far East Square
Singapore 048763

Library of Congress Control Number 2009930848

British Library Cataloguing in Publication data

A catalogue record for this book is available from the British Library

ISBN 978-1-4129-4772-5
ISBN 978-1-4129-4773-2 (pbk)

Typeset by C&M Digitals (P) Ltd, Chennai, India
Printed in Great Britain by CPI Antony Rowe, Chippenham, Wiltshire
Printed on paper from sustainable resources

Mixed Sources
Product group from well-managed
forests and other controlled sources
www.fsc.org Cert no. SGS-COC-2953
© 1996 Forest Stewardship Council
FSC

Education at SAGE

SAGE is a leading international publisher of journals, books, and electronic media for academic, educational, and professional markets.

Our education publishing includes:

- accessible and comprehensive texts for aspiring education professionals and practitioners looking to further their careers through continuing professional development

- inspirational advice and guidance for the classroom

- authoritative state of the art reference from the leading authors in the field

Find out more at: **www.sagepub.co.uk/education**

Contents

Acknowledgements

This book would not have been written without the encouragement of so many people that I cannot begin to thank them all.

My thanks must however go to Sue East and Jane Chesters, who encouraged my own vision so many years ago, and to Anke Bauer, Paula Coates, Pamela Alexander and Pat Andrews who have been with me in mind or spirit all the way.

A big thank you to the dedicated Learning Mentors at Plashet School, London.

Thank you to Jude Bowen for her patience, and to Amy Jarrold for being at the end of the phone.

Thank you to my parents.

About the Author

Stephanie George is a teacher in London. She was a Learning Mentor from 1999 to 2003 in a large urban secondary school, but she trained originally as a Careers Guidance Practitioner having gained a Masters in Guidance and Education Management.

In 2003 she set up a Learning Support Unit and became involved in training Learning Mentors, sharing good practice and leading successful mentoring teams. Stephanie is also an independent trainer and is particularly interested in the impact of Learning Mentor intervention upon student achievement.

Stephanie can be seen in action on Teachers TV at http://www.teachers.tv/video/34722

How to Use this Book

The role of the mentor already has an extensive body of work supporting its activity. Numerous books and studies offer definitions of mentoring and there are award winning mentoring schemes around the world from which we can gain an understanding of successful and effective strategies. The work of a Learning Mentor, however, is different; the educational context has a set of complex and target-driven demands with the achievement of young people at its heart.

Setting up, developing and organising a Learning Mentor team should be carefully handled and there are three essential things to consider:

- how the Learning Mentor will fit into the structure and vision of the school

- how the Learning Mentor will function within the school

- how the impact of the Learning Mentor will be measured.

A Learning Mentor team that is set up without a clear understanding of its function and role within the school can compromise the outcome, and it is important to set out at the start for teachers, parents and students what the role of the mentor encompasses.

The objectives of this book are to enable school leaders, trainers, parents, teachers, governors and Learning Mentors to:

- understand the benefit to the whole school of having a team of Learning Mentors

- be clear about the aims, purpose and objectives of the role of the Learning Mentor within the school

- explore a range of referral methods, mentoring models and methods of intervention when working with young people and children in overcoming barriers to learning

- understand the importance and sensitivity of working with young people, their carers and parents, teachers and other professionals within the context of the whole school

- explore the role of the Learning Mentor as an emerging profession within schools, and to consider the elements of professionalism that distinguish the formal mentoring role from an informal mentoring relationship

- be clear about the necessity for appropriate case management and monitoring

- provide evidence of the impact of intervention.

There are figures and activities to use with each chapter, to help the reader develop some of the ideas within the book. At the end of many of the chapters there are suggestions for further reading in the form of books or useful websites.

The aims of this book are to:

- encourage Learning Mentors to think about their role as professional Learning Mentor Practitioners and the successful management of a caseload of student mentees

- help schools ensure that they have a clear vision and understanding of the work of Learning Mentors, and how Learning Mentors work with children and young people to help overcome barriers to learning

- help the reader develop knowledge about the process of mentoring, and the range of interventions that can assist young people and children within schools

- help teachers, parents, carers and school staff to gain an understanding of the role of the Learning Mentor, as distinct from that of informal mentoring

- encourage schools to develop professional Learning Mentor teams within a formal structure, thus enabling students to access the best possible range of formal mentoring intervention so that they can maximise their potential.

A note on the text

Throughout the book, the term school has been used to represent any setting where a Learning Mentor is working.

List of Downloadable Material

Wherever you see the [icon] icon downloadable material can be found at www.sagepub.co.uk/george for use in your setting. For a full list please see below.

Chapter 1   The Educational Context

Functional Map for the Provision of Learning Mentor Services
Learning Mentor Functions Focusing Activity
Functional Map Criteria (Complementary Service)
Functional Map Criteria (Mentoring Relationships)
Functional Map Criteria (Networks and Partnerships)
Functional Map Criteria (Managing and Promoting Provision)
Reflective Questions – Developing Professionalism
Raising the Profile of Learning Mentors

Chapter 2   Learning Mentors – Fitting into the Setting

Knowing your School Activity – Pastoral
Knowing your School Activity – Organisational
Learning Mentor Team Development Plan
Learning Mentors and Every Child Matters Mapping

Chapter 3   Getting Ready to Mentor

Preparing to Mentor Checklist
Referral to Learning Mentor
Request for Learning Mentor Intervention
Sample Letter to Parents 1
Sample Letter to Parents 2
Sample Letter to Parents 3
Step by Step Guide to the First Mentoring Appointment
I SEE Matrix – a Model for Learning Mentoring

Chapter 4   Partnerships with Internal and External Agencies

What are the Referral Procedures for Contacting External Agencies?

Chapter 5   Accountability and Monitoring

'What if?' Mentoring Cards
Student Self-Assessment Form
Target Setting and Action Plan
Learning Mentor Tracking Sheet
Learning Mentor Student Evaluation Form

Chapter 6   Keeping it Going

Learning Mentor Awareness
Personalised Map of Opportunities to Promote and Embed Learning Mentor
Provision

1

The Educational Context

> **This chapter covers:**
>
> - **The role of the Learning Mentor in a school**
> - **Learning Mentors as professionals**
> - **Raising the profile of the Learning Mentor**

Issues around teaching and learning are so well documented that there are a huge range of resources, journals, publications, theory and practice to help teachers to share good practice, garner advice and share ideas to draw upon in terms of making lessons engaging and interesting. Teachers are familiar with the need to keep lessons pacey and to offer opportunities for students to show what they can do. Peer assessment and evaluation are high on the agenda and independent learning is encouraged.

However, where does the Learning Mentor look for similar guidance? I think that we can in fact draw comparisons to the role of the NQT, the newly qualified teacher. There is a broad quality assured induction package programme with professional skills and knowledge that must be assessed. What induction package do we offer to Learning Mentors as professional practitioners? Can we be sure that the same levels of professional practice are adhered to, are explicit and that there is parity of standards? We know that OfSTED have critically evaluated the impact of Learning Mentor practice and their findings answer the question quite emphatically as follows:

> Learning mentors are making a significant effect on the attendance, behaviour, self-esteem and progress of the pupils they support ... the most successful and highly valued strand of the EiC [Excellence in Cities] programme ... In 95% of the survey schools, inspectors judged that the mentoring programme made a positive contribution to the mainstream provision of the school as a whole, and had a beneficial effect on the behaviour of individual pupils and on their ability to learn and make progress. (OfSTED, 2003: 46)

Clearly evidence suggests that Learning Mentors are effective and having an impact. What we need to do is ensure consistent practice. The Learning

Mentor's role is now fully supported by a clear qualification structure, developed by the Department for Children, Schools and Families (DCSF). The role is categorised as one of the family of professionals who belong to the group known as 'Learning Development and Support Services for Children, Young People and Those Who Care for Them'. The National Occupational Standards provide clear guidance about the functions of the Learning Mentor, the professional qualifications and the context in which the role is appropriate. The qualifications framework and standards makes explicit the context of the role and its relationship to other complementary and similar roles that involve the support of children and young people, for example personal advisors for Connexions. The qualifications framework provides a bundle of units that help to induct the Learning Mentor and clearly defines the knowledge, skills and qualities that are required for the developing practitioner.

The units are mapped against a value base thus facilitating comparison and equivalence. Learning Mentors are also established as part of the new Children's Workforce, and are supported through the new Children's Workforce Development Council (CWDC). The CWDC describes the role of the Learning Mentor as being 'To provide support and guidance to children, young people and those engaged with them, by removing barriers to learning in order to promote effective participation, enhance individual learning, raise aspirations and achieve their potential' (www.cwdcouncil.org.uk/learning-mentors).

The functional map for the provision of Learning Mentor services is a very good place to start in terms of looking at the functions of the Learning Mentor and the skills that will be required for the Learning Mentor to provide successful intervention within the school setting.

What does all this mean for you in your school and how can you be sure that you are meeting the requirements and functions of a Learning Mentor by working holistically within the framework of the school to support children and young people? A good place to start is to look at what you currently do in your school. What interventions and activities are Learning Mentors involved in at your school? A useful task is to map those interventions and activities against the functional map.

 Activity

Using the 'Learning Mentor Functions Focusing Activity' Sheet, make a list of all of the activities that the Learning Mentor(s) is (are) involved in.

Think carefully about when you run these activities, for example the time of day, day of the week, week of the term and term in the year. Think also about seasonal things, for example religious festivals, annual events, celebrations and seasonal aspects of the school year.

Functional Map for the Provision of Learning Mentor Services

A definition of learning mentoring: To provide support and guidance to children, young people and those engaged with them, by removing barriers to learning in order to promote effective participation, enhance individual learning, raise aspirations and achieve their potential.

Learning Mentor services should provide a complementary service, which enhances existing provision in order to support learning, participation and encourage social inclusion.	Assist children and young people to make a successful transfer between educational establishments and transition at key stages in their learning.
	Contribute to the comprehensive assessment of children and young people entering educational establishments and the review of their progress and achievements.
	Contribute to the identification of barriers to learning for individual children and young people and provide them with a range of strategies for overcoming the barriers.
Learning Mentor services should aim to develop and maintain effective and supportive mentoring relationships with children and young people and those engaged with them.	Establish and develop effective one-to-one mentoring and other supportive relationships with children and young people.
	Develop, agree and implement a time bound action plan with groups and individual children and young people and those involved with them based on a comprehensive assessment of their strengths and needs.
	Facilitate access to specialist support services for children and young people with barriers to learning.
	Assist in the identification of early signs of disengagement and contribute to specific interventions to encourage re-engagement.
	Operate within agreed legal, ethical and professional boundaries when working with children and young people and those involved with them.
Learning Mentors should work within an extended range of networks and partnerships to broker support and learning opportunities and improve the quality of services to children and young people.	Develop and maintain appropriate contact with the families and carers of children and young people who have identified needs.
	Negotiate, establish and maintain effective working partnerships with other agencies and individuals in order to address needs and help remove barriers to learning for children and young people.
	Contribute to the identification and sharing of good practice between individuals and partner agencies to enhance mentoring provision.
Leaming Mentors should manage and promote Leaming Mentor provision and raise standards of service.	Develop a policy that will promote inclusion, achievement and personal development of students.
	Work within the organisation to integrate Learning Mentor provision and co-ordinate such support within existing provision.
	To ensure that Leaming Mentor provision is appropriately monitored, reviewed and evaluated to ensure effective practice.

Photocopiable:

The Learning Mentor Manual © Stephanie George, 2010.

Learning Mentor Functions Focusing Activity

Autumn Term 1	
Autumn Term 2	
Spring Term 3	
Spring Term 4	
Summer Term 5	
Summer Term 6	

You should end up with an overview of the Learning Mentor input across the school year. You might discover a particular strength, or there may be areas to develop. You might discover that resources need to be redirected, or that in fact there is a good balance of activities and interventions across the year, or that you might want to deepen or embed the intervention or the range of activities in one particular part of the school.

Functional Skills Mapping

In order to develop the functions of the learning mentor the next step would be to look at the activities and tasks and map them against the functional map. I have provided some thinking prompts to help you with the categorisation of the tasks and mapping these against the functional skills.

1. Functional skill number 1 is to provide a complementary service which enhances existing provision, in order to support learning, participation and encourage social inclusion.

Thinking Prompt:

-   How do you provide this complementary service as described in functional skill number 1 – do you have a Breakfast Club, what extra curricular activities does the school offer?

-   How accessible are your activities?

-   How do you link in with other departments in the school?

-   Are other departments aware of what you do in the school?

-   How do you publicise the activities?

-   Are you doing more of the same or are you offering something that is different to other departments?

2. Functional skill number 2 is to develop and maintain effective and supportive mentoring relationships with children and young people and those engaged with them.

Thinking Prompt:

-   Are students aware of how to make contact with you (appropriate times, location, access)?

-   Where, when and how does mentoring take place?

- How is mentoring introduced to students?

- How is baseline assessment conducted?

- How do you refer to external agencies?

- What protocols exist if/when referrals need to be made?

- What training is in place for Learning Mentors?

- What provision is made for Continuing Professional Development?

- How are parents involved in the mentoring process?

- What presence do mentors have at open evenings/parents' evenings/ transition events?

3. Functional skill number 3 aims to ensure that Learning Mentors work within an extended range of networks and partnerships to broker support and learning opportunities and improve the quality of services to children and young people.

Thinking Prompt:

- What partnerships do you have with other organisations? List the organisations.

- How accessible are they to you as a mentor or team of mentors?

- Do you publicise other learning opportunities, e.g. summer holiday schemes, youth club activities, young carers' networks?

- How do you make people aware of your links with other organisations?

- Do you have a leaflet display area that staff and students can access?

- Do you use ICT to maximise your access to contacts and keep yourself organised?

- Which network events/meetings do you attend?

- Who do you work in partnership with in the school (think about the following: School Police Liaison Officer, Child Protection Officer, Attendance Officer, School Social Worker, and School Nurse)?

4. Functional skill number 4 is concerned with the skills necessary for the Learning Mentors to manage and promote learning mentor provision and raise standards of service.

Thinking Prompt:

- Have you contributed to the school policy with regard to Learning Mentor Practice?

- Does the policy need review?

- Does the policy reflect developments, progress within practice?

- Do you evaluate Learning Mentor practice/provision?

- How do you obtain feedback on the effectiveness of Learning Mentor provision within the school?

- How well are the interventions working?

- What impact is Learning Mentor intervention having with the school?

- How can you demonstrate effectiveness?

- Are parents, students, governors and teachers aware of the work interventions and activities provided by Learning Mentors?

- How well integrated is Learning Mentor support and processes with other provision?

I have provided a set of frames ('Functional Map Criteria' Forms 1–4) for you to work through this activity, with headings, so that you can begin the work of evaluating your organisation's mentoring intervention.

You should end up with a pretty good picture of your activities mapped against the Functional Map, and you should easily be able to see any imbalances or gaps. This exercise really helps to identify strengths in your team, and to seek out areas that need development so that you can meet the needs of your students in your setting. You can then use this knowledge to plan for the future, perhaps the next academic year in the medium to long term. In the short term you might decide that you can shift resources to another intervention or activity that may have more immediate impact or on the other hand, seek to embed and promote longevity.

Finally this activity will provide you with a document that is extremely useful in terms of preparing the following documents:

- A Learning Mentor Policy

- A Learning Mentor Handbook

- A departmental Handbook

1. Functional Map Criteria (Complementary Service)

At this school Learning Mentors provide a complementary service which enhances existing provision in order to support learning, participation and encourage social inclusion by:

2. Functional Map Criteria (Mentoring Relationships)

At this school we develop and maintain effective and supportive mentoring relationships with children and young people and those engaged with them by:

3. Functional Map Criteria (Networks and Partnerships)

At this school Learning Mentors work within an extended range of networks and partnerships to broker support and learning opportunities and improve the quality of services to children and young people by:

4. Functional Map Criteria (Managing and Promoting Provision)

At this school Learning Mentors manage and promote Learning Mentor provision and raise standards of service by:

National Occupational Standards	
Learning Mentor Formal Qualification Structure National Vocational Qualification Level 3 Scottish National Vocational Qualification Level 3	
Compulsory Units	• Contribute to the protection of children and young people from abuse
	• Ensure your own actions reduce risks to health and safety
	• Review own contribution to the service
	• Enable children and young people to find out about and use services and facilities
	• Operate within networks
Two Learning Mentor Specific Units	• Facilitate children and young people's learning and development through mentoring
	• Support the child or young person's successful transfer and transition in learning and development contexts
Plus 2 further units from a range of optional units which vary upon the choice of training provider	

Figure 1.1   National Occupational Standards NVLQ3

- A set of procedures

- Information for the whole school Handbook.

Learning Mentors as Professionals in Schools

Workforce remodelling has had a significant impact upon the way schools work. There exists now a broad range of staff within schools who have a range of different skills, qualifications and expertise that can make an important contribution to the whole school ethos and approach, for example, the School Nurse, the Educational Welfare Officer, School Social Workers and Teaching Assistants. Most if not all of these roles will have their own qualifications and skills structure that are particular to those professions. The National Occupational Standards for the Learning, Development and Support Services (NOS LDSS) specifically address training for Learning Mentors. Many schools will have their own school specific general induction package for all new staff, this is likely to be followed with mentor specific training and/or development for experienced Learning Mentors. This training may be within the school itself led by a Lead Mentor, or at borough or county level where a group of mentors are trained on a training day perhaps. Training may take the form of short focused sessions, half day sessions, full day training or indeed a series of training sessions.

Let's look specifically now at the The National Occupational Standards for the Learning, Development and Support Services (NOS LDSS). There

National Occupational Standards		
Learning Mentor Formal Qualification Structure National Vocational Qualification Level 4 Scottish National Vocational Qualification Level 4		
Compulsory Units	Ensure personal safety and security	
	Evaluate and develop own contribution to the service	
	Develop interactions with clients	
	Develop and sustain arrangements for joint working between workers and agencies	
	Promote and maximise educational opportunities and achievements for individual children and young people	
Two Learning Mentor Specific Units	Manage personal case load	
	Challenge systems and processes that are failing	
Plus 3 further units from a range of optional units which vary upon the choice of training provider		

Figure 1.2   National Occupational Standards NVLQ4

are National Vocational Qualifications (NVQs) at Levels 3 and 4, and Foundation Degrees, giving status, rigour and credibility to Learning Mentor training and indeed creating a professional set of standards by which Learning Mentors are measured. The qualifications seek to provide a strong foundation for practice and resonate with the functional skills. As can be seen from the overview of the qualifications given in Figures 1.1 and 1.2 the qualifications make clear the need for Learning Mentors to provide a service that offers information, support and guidance to young people and specifically to action plan, review, and assist children and young people, and to support the learning and development of children and young people. The qualifications also provide a level of quality assurance for Learning Mentors, trainers, schools, colleges and organisations.

Learning Mentors come to the role from a variety of backgrounds with a range of previous experiences. It is not uncommon to have Learning Mentors who come from a guidance or personal advisor background, or a learning support role, or they may have recently graduated. With the recent growth of the profession, new roles such as Senior, Lead or Cluster Lead Mentor roles are now emerging. The new Foundation Degrees build on the NVQ qualifications, offering clear progressional routes giving opportunities for further study if desired.

Opportunities for training at a local level of course cannot be underestimated, and it is here that local knowledge, understanding and expertise are crucial as nothing can replace knowing one's school, parents and community well. It is vitally important to take every opportunity to attend and become involved in local network briefings, meetings and events, local INSET (In Service Education and Training) and opportunities for CPD, as well as meeting and linking with local Learning Mentors. Keeping in touch with the local Lead Co-ordinator is also extremely useful, as they have an overview of the provision at local level and can bring the advantages, skills and experience that such an overview involves. This is so important in developing an understanding of the needs of your organisation and locality, and thus contributes to the knowledge that a Learning Mentor must acquire if they are to meet the needs of their students. It allows them to develop the crucial professional knowledge and skills required in their role.

Becoming a Professional

What are the qualities of professionalism? A few things come to mind:

- Appropriate training and substantial specialist knowledge.

- Competence and skills in their field, along with a commitment to life-long Continuing Professional Development (CPD).

- Personal high standards, with self-reflection and self-management.

- Accountability for what you do, and how you do it.

- Being open to monitoring.

- Understanding confidentiality and appropriate professional behaviour.

- Respect and care for the young people and children that you work with.

A useful activity might be to look at your school and the professionalism or developing professionalism of the Learning Mentor provision within it. It might be helpful to conduct this activity together with all the Learning Mentors in your school, your line manager and perhaps a member of staff who is outside the department and can offer an objective view. Make some time to do this; sit down with a cup of tea, and go through your provision step by step with a view to improving and developing the provision in your school with openness and transparency. It will help to plan the development of the Learning Mentor provision from a clear evidence base.

Professionalism on a Day-to-Day Basis

On a daily basis what does professionalism mean for the Learning Mentor and the school? I think it means doing what you say you will do, when you say you are going to do it, with positive regard for the children and young people you work with, and with the help and support of the other professionals within the organisation. This means:

- keeping appointments with students at the scheduled times

- starting and organising clubs and groups on time, and in an orderly fashion

- keeping clear records of any interventions, for reference

- planning and preparing for groups or clubs, and ensuring the appropriate resources are available

- having a clear plan of what you are going to do with any particular group, and paying attention to the objectives and outcomes

- reviewing interventions periodically, and assessing and reassessing effectiveness

- listening to advice and guidance from fellow professionals and colleagues

- knowing, understanding and giving due regard to the policies of the school, most importantly child protection and anti-bullying

- being appropriately dressed (your school may have a formal dress code, find out what it is and abide by it)

- effective communication with a range of audiences, including students, governors and parents

- using diplomacy, tact and humour coupled with the ability to diffuse potentially difficult situations where there is a risk of conflict

- working well within teams, be it year teams, departments or the whole school.

Consideration of these aspects of professonalism is important for ensuring both the competence and effectiveness of the Learning Mentor provision and a positive perception of the provision within the organisation.

Take some time now to think about the Learning Mentor in your organisation. 'Reflective Questions: Developing Professionalism' is a self reflective exercise for a Learning Mentor to reflect on their approach to mentoring. The activity can also be applicable to other staff in the organisation thinking about the current provision and how they would answer these questions.

Reflective Questions – Developing Professionalism

What does my mentoring interview approach convey to students?

What does my mentoring approach convey to other staff in the school?

How do I engage with students at the first mentoring meeting?

In what ways do I engage with parents?

What do students understand about my role?

What do teachers understand about my role?

Are expectations clear to students?

Skills of the Learning Mentor

I have discussed the role of the Learning Mentor, the qualifications structure and the expectations and although the qualifications are clear in their outcomes I will outline here what I consider to be the necessary skills a Learning Mentor must possess:

- the ability to listen well

- good verbal communication

- good written communication

- an ability to build up a good rapport with students (and colleagues and parents)

- a desire to work with young people

- the ability to paraphrase and summarise

- an awareness of body language and non-verbal communication

- an appreciation that mentoring is not a 'quick fix'

- reliability, patience and resilience

- the ability to be calm in a crisis

- being a good record keeper.

All of these skills and qualities will help the Learning Mentor to help the young people they are working with, and good communication and reliability both stand out to me as invaluable assets for Learning Mentors working with young people who so often need the stability and understanding that the Learning Mentor role can provide.

Raising the profile of Learning Mentors within the School

Raising the profile and keeping up the momentum for Learning Mentors is a job that needs planning and attention, and it goes hand in hand with maintaining a professional approach.

I have provided a completed example of an overview of ways in which we can begin thinking about raising the profile of Learning Mentors within organisations. This particular example is a tried and tested example from a secondary school – see Figure 1.3.

I have also provided a blank sample that can be worked through for any setting and then finalised and used as part of the Learning Mentor Handbook.

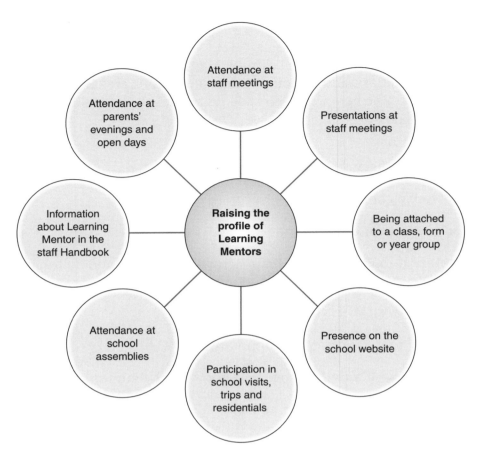

Figure 1.3   Ways of Raising the Profile of Learning Mentors

It will provide a very clear overview of how the Learning Mentor can raise their profile and keep it buoyant in the organisation. Once this activity has been done, it just needs to be updated each year.

Key points

1. Undertaking a review of the Functional Skills required for mentoring and a review of the current mentoring interventions within your school is a useful way to identify successes and areas for improvement.
2. Identifying the strengths in provision, and the areas for development with the mentoring team, are important stages in improving provision.
3. Thinking about the qualifications structure and the role of professionalism within Learning Mentor practice is an essential part of being a professional.
4. The range of activities you offer as a Learning Mentor Team will help to raise the Learning Mentor Team profile within the school.
5. The development of a self evaluation tool is an essential part of facilitating good practice.

Ways of Raising the Profile of Learning Mentors

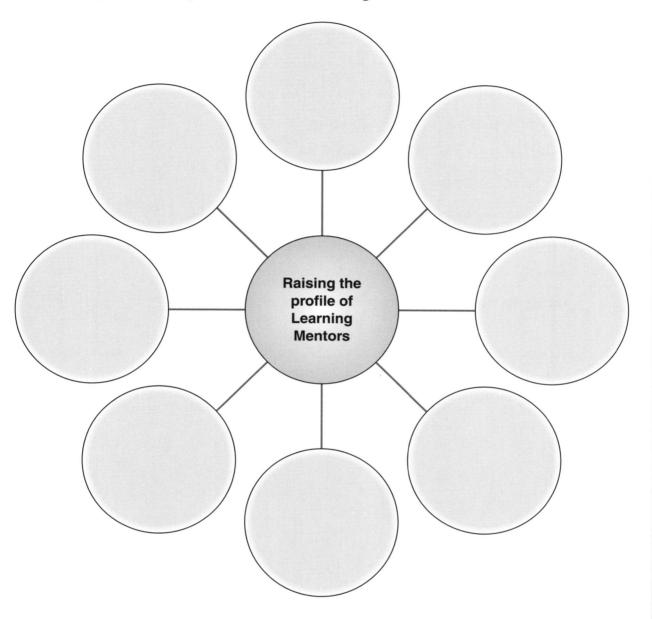

Raising the profile of Learning Mentors

Downloadable material

Go to www.sagepub.co.uk/george for downloadable material to this chapter.

Functional Map for the Provision of Learning Mentor Services

Learning Mentor Functions Focusing Activity

Functional Map Criteria (Complementary Service)

Functional Map Criteria (Mentoring Relationships)

Functional Map Criteria (Networks and Partnerships)

Functional Map Criteria (Managing and Promoting Provision)

Reflective Questions – Developing Professionalism

Raising the Profile of Learning Mentors

Further reading

Department for Education and Employment (DfEE) (1999) *Excellence in Cities 1999*. London: DfEE Publications.

2

Learning Mentors – Fitting into the Setting

> **This chapter covers:**
>
> - **How Learning Mentors fit into the school or setting**
> - **Learning Mentors and the Every Child Matters agenda**
> - **Getting to know your school**

Conducting a Learning Walk

There are a number of educational contexts where Learning Mentors can be found, most usually within primary schools, secondary schools, Further Education colleges, the Youth Service and Pupil Referral Units. Fitting into the systems and working practices of the school or setting is very important for the success of the provision and ensuring that the needs of the young people and children are met. One of the first things a Learning Mentor will need to do is get to know the organisation. This is essential, as it creates a starting point for thinking about ways to engage with the variety of people and groups within the organisation. A structured approach to this makes things less haphazard, and getting to know your organisation by taking a 'learning walk' around it and finding and talking to people is the method I recommend. Use the resource sheets 'Knowing your School Activity – Pastoral and Organisational' as a guide.

Here is a tried and tested approach to use and adapt for your setting.

Knowing your School Activity – Pastoral

Take a Learning Walk, using the template below, to find out how your school is organised

Getting to Know your School – Pastoral and Curriculum

Number of form classes per year group and their names	EAL Team	
Heads of Year/House and office location	Child Protection key staff	
Senior Management Team and roles	Looked After Children	
SENCO (Special Educational Needs/Inclusion & Learning Support)	Extra Curricular /Extended Schools	
Primary/ Secondary Transition	Librarians/Learning Resource & Study Support	

Knowing your School Activity – Organisational

Take a Learning Walk, using the template below, to find out how your school is organised

Getting to Know your School – Organisational and Domestic

		CPD Co-ordinator	
Staff Governors			
Site Supervisors Keys Access to building Parking		AVA/Media Resources	
ICT/Computers/Passwords/ email		Personnel matters and pay	
Union Representatives		Finance and ordering	

Photocopiable:
The Learning Mentor Manual © Stephanie George, 2010.

> **Activity**
>
> Attach the resource sheet to your clipboard, and take a couple of pencils with you. Start with the school receptionist or main office staff during lesson time, as they will be less busy during lessons; ask them for a telephone list, staff list and a map of the school. Check the timetable if you can, and try to establish which departments have quieter periods at which particular times of the day or week, then you can approach people when they should be under less pressure. Get to the staff room five minutes before break, because if teachers are not teaching before break they may well go to the staff room early and you may be able to catch them then. As you walk around the school, you will become familiar with faces, classrooms, departmental areas, offices, and get a feel for the movement around the school. Do not forget to step outside the school buildings and get a sense of where the school sits in its community.

The Aims, Vision and Mission of the Organisation

The task of getting to know your school by walking around it and talking to the staff will help you to become familiar with your school as it operates on a daily basis. However, it's just as important to look at the aims, vision and mission of the school. There are some key questions you must have the answers for, such as:

- Where is the school going?

- What are the medium and long term aims?

- What does the school hope to achieve?

- How does the school hope to achieve its targets?

To get an answer to all of these questions, and to the many others that will no doubt have been triggered by your learning walk, you will need to develop a sound understanding of the school and its aims. A good way to begin to get an idea of the position of the school is to read the most recent OfSTED Inspection Report. I would suggest that you obtain a copy (this can be found on the OfSTED website), and make some time to read it, and if time allows that you read the last two or three OfSTED reports. This will give you an opportunity to detect trends, any areas of difficulty and any areas of strength. It will help you get a feel for the school, its students and their needs. This snapshot provides a starting point for understanding the direction of the school, and I think often reveals much about its ethos. Look at any action points suggested by the OfSTED Inspectors, and find out if these have been acted upon when you look at subsequent OfSTED reports. You might well discover more about the school's commitment to a particular area, for example inclusion, working with parents or working with the community. Does the school have strengths in the area of study support, what key improvements have been made and where else does the school need to go to improve? The OfSTED report will certainly guide and inform you, but it is only a starting point, and you should make a point of looking at the following:

- The School Profile

- The School Prospectus

- The School's website

- The School Development Plan

- School Handbook

- Latest Newsletter to parents

- Latest Report to the governing body

Obtain these documents, read them, become familiar with them and refer to them again and again if you need to. The approach taken by the Learning Mentor team must work within the school structure, and chime with its aims, so it is vital that Learning Mentors understand the direction of the school and how things are done there.

The Learning Mentor Policy

A policy will need to be developed for the Learning Mentor practice within the school. The policy needs to outline the philosophy and procedures for Learning Mentoring within the school. The policy will be shaped by the school's ethos and approach to inclusion and supportive interventions, and needs to explain the aims and purpose of the Learning Mentoring in the school. It should consider the following:

- What will the approach be?

- How and when will children be seen for mentoring?

- What are the processes for referral?

- How will evaluation take place?

- How will reporting back to parents take place?

- How will staff be kept informed?

- What is the criteria for referral to Learning Mentors?

- What are the exit procedures/how will mentoring end?

- How will student progress be monitored?

- If necessary, how will referrals be made to external agencies?

All of these questions need to be addressed by the policy, and I have provided tools for developing responses to all of these factors, starting with the Learning Mentor Development Plan.

The Learning Mentor Development Plan

When developing a plan that will help to steer the approach for Learning Mentoring within the school, and to help to formulate your policy, consideration needs to be given to the following:

- In what ways will the Learning Mentoring fit into the School Development Plan?

- Are there any aspects of the School Development Plan that Learning Mentors can directly contribute to?

- Are there any opportunities for working with other departments to develop any particular aspects of the School Development Plan?

- Are there aspects of Learning Mentoring that can be developed further to provide synergy with the School Development Plan?

- Is the Learning Mentoring provision appropriately focused, and if not what needs to be changed or adapted?

By taking a critical view of the Learning Mentor practice with the School Development Plan, you can ensure that mentoring is not happening in isolation from other interventions taking place within the school. Developing the Learning Mentor development plan in this way makes the task simpler and clearer, and it also provides a level of quality assurance as the Learning Mentor development plan emerges as it is informed by the School Development Plan.

I would make the plan fairly simple for the sake of transparency. See the 'Learning Mentor Team Development Plan' outline, included here, that you can adapt or use directly for your setting.

Learning Mentor Team Development Plan			
Development Plan objectives ⟶			
Action (What needs to be done)			
Key staff (Who will do it)			
How (How it will be done)			
Resources (What resources will be needed to get it done)			
Evidence of success (How will you know we have met our initial aims?)			

 Photocopiable:

The Learning Mentor Manual © Stephanie George, 2010.

Every Child Matters

The Every Child Matters outcomes have particular relevance for Learning Mentors; this can be seen by identifying commonalities between the outcomes of Every Child Matters and the Learning Mentor Functional Map. Figure 2.1 shows how Learning Mentors fit in with the Every Child Matters outcomes. Turning now to your organisation and context look through the range of activities that you currently provide for your students; a useful activity is to look at how well these are mapped against the Every Child Matters outcomes. The resource sheet, 'Learning Mentors and Every Child Matters Outcomes' provides an opportunity to map current activities, clubs, groups, in fact all learning mentor activity, against the outcomes. I have provided space for four interventions in each category but depending on your organisation, its size, your departmental priorities and direction, you might want to have just one main activity for each of the outcomes or indeed two, three, four or more. It really depends upon your context. The main thing is that once you have completed this mapping activity you will have a useful document to include in your departmental handbook, staff handbook or similar.

Key Policies for Learning Mentors

Looking at the Every Child Matters outcomes brings me to the breadth of interventions that are involved and also makes it apparent that Learning Mentors need a good grasp of some significant policies within the organisation, in particular the following:

- Child Protection Policy and procedures

- Confidentiality Policy or procedures

- Anti-bullying Policy

- Special Educational Needs Policy

- Inclusion Policy or statement

- Behaviour Policy

- Attendance and Punctuality Policy

- Exclusion Policy

Learning Mentors should ensure that they have knowledge of these policies, are aware of the procedures related to them and have easy access to them on a day-to-day basis. It is sometimes the case that mentors find themselves in the position of dealing with a crisis situation, it is therefore imperative that matters are handled sensitively, correctly and with due care and regard for the policies and procedures related thereto.

Stay safe	Be healthy	Achieve economic well-being	Make a positive contribution	Enjoy and achieve
Working with students to help them make positive decisions	Running breakfast clubs	Provide support and guidance for young people entering the world of work	Develop self confidence	Work with students on issues relating to attendance
Supporting interventions with students on issues relating to bullying	Making provision for holiday clubs and activities outside of term time	Work with students making post-16 decisions around college and course options	Provide opportunities for students to improve attitude to learning	Assist students to identify barriers to learning
Identify and act appropriately with regard to child protection issues	Work with students to help them understand conflict situations and deal with them appropriately	Support families to support the young person in education	Provide support to assist students in achieving targets	Make provision for homework clubs
Work with Learning Mentor on issues relating to conflict resolution	Making provision for activities during play, break and lunchtimes	Assist students with budgeting	Support students with interventions to support self esteem	Support students on issues relating to punctuality

Figure 2.1 Learning Mentors and Every Child Matters Outcomes

Learning Mentors and Every Child Matters Mapping

Learning Mentors and Every Child Matters Outcomes

Stay safe	Be Healthy	Achieve economic well-being	Make a positive contribution	Enjoy and achieve

The School Office

The staff in the school office are a conduit to every avenue of the school. The staff there can help you with everything, from finding a child, time-tables, welfare issues and more. They know which parents can be a little tricky, and will guide you well. They know who to ask and when to ask if you need something quickly. Get to know them all by name and do it quickly, and if you look after them they will look after you. Finally, it helps to know your school receptionist very well indeed.

Key points

- Conducting a 'learning walk' in your school allows you to get a feel for the organisation and how it work on a daily basis, whilst examining key documents facilitates thinking around the school's development, aims, objectives and strategic direction.
- The creation, development or review of the Learning Mentor Team's Development Plan brings coherence to the provision and should work in harmony with the School Development Plan.
- Mapping the Learning Mentor tasks and activities against the Every Child Matters outcomes brings clarity and facilitates a review of interventions.
- Learning Mentors need a good understanding of all school policies and procedures, but those around inclusion, behaviour, child protection, and anti-bullying need particularly close attention.

Downloadable material

Go to www.sagepub.co.uk/george for downloadable material resources to this chapter.

Knowing your School Activity – Pastoral

Knowing your School Activity – Organisational

Learning Mentor Team Development Plan

Learning Mentors and Every Child Matters Mapping

Further reading

Department for Education and Skills (DfES) (2004) *Every Child Matters: Change for Children*. London: DfES.

3

Getting Ready to Mentor

This chapter covers:

- **What is mentoring?**
- **The referral process**
- **The mentoring relationship**
- **The range of mentoring interventions that can be applied**
- **Confidentiality and Learning Mentors**

What is Mentoring?

One of the things to consider is a definition of mentoring. A definition that may be useful in the context of examining the work of Learning Mentors is one that describes mentoring as a 'process in which one person (mentor) is responsible for overseeing the career and development of another person (protégé) outside the normal manager/subordinate relationship' (Clutterbuck, 1999).

Learning Mentors will essentially do the same outside the normal teacher/student relationship but with one main difference, that difference being the role of the Learning Mentor is a formal one within an educational setting.

In most cases, the mentee/learner is referred to the Learning Mentor by a member of staff. The process of formal referral compromises the voluntary nature of the natural mentor and gives it a very precise focus within the school environment. It is this that is at the heart of the Learning Mentor function. The Learning Mentor's approach must be one of facilitator, guide, supporter, enabler and even sometimes advocate. The role is not one of a friend, or of a manager.

We need to be clear about what the day-to-day activity of mentoring is, and so below is a summary of the work that a Learning Mentor may find themselves doing:

- working with children and young people to identify any barriers to learning

- working with children and young people to develop an action plan for moving forward

- target setting around issues such as behaviour and attendance

- making provision for students to work on coursework, homework, revision and study skills

- offering guidance and support with personal and domestic issues

- providing opportunities for students to develop self-esteem and confidence

- working collaboratively with other professionals to support children, young people and their parents and carers

- co-ordinating, developing and running groups on issues such as conflict mediation, anger management and similar

- contributing to and making provision for holiday clubs and activities.

Looking at this overview of Learning Mentor activities and interventions, it's clear that Learning Mentor activities can generally be described as falling into two categories, firstly individual one-to-one work with students that I will call casework, and group activities that include workshops, groups sessions, after school clubs and holiday activities which I will call group work. The principles remain the same for both.

Learning Mentors and Working with Students

When working with children and young people, we need to develop a carefully planned and considered approach. It is important that we do this from the initial meeting with the student, as this is the foundation upon which the mentoring relationship is built. Important qualities for the Learning Mentor to consider are their own professional skills and practice, as mentioned in Chapter 1. These professional skills come into play when establishing the relationship with the student, parents or carers, teachers and other staff in the school, as well as external partners working with the child and/or family. Gathering some key facts before meeting with the student is vital. Use the 'Preparing to Mentor Checklist' as a guide to help you with this.

It can also form the basis of your case file for the student. If it is kept at the front of the student's file, it will serve as a quick and easy reference checklist

Preparing to Mentor Checklist

	Activity	Completed
1.	Name of student being mentored	
2.	Form class and form tutor name	
3.	Print basic data from SIMS student	
4.	Obtain parent/carer consent to mentor	
5.	Obtain attendance and punctuality history	
6.	Obtain any medical information that may be relevant	
7.	Discuss the reasons for the referral with the referrer (this may be the form tutor/head of year/class teacher or similar)	
	Now you are ready to make the appointment to see the student.	

Photocopiable:

The Learning Mentor Manual © Stephanie George, 2010.

for key names, contact details, the class the student is in and so on, and this can be very useful when information is needed in a hurry. If dates are added as and when the checklist is completed, then a clear historical picture is also created and this is a simple way to track progress. Computer casework records are an absolute necessity these days particularly as they facilitate monitoring and statistical analysis and I will talk about this in detail in Chapter 5, but a handy accessible paper record like this checklist is always a boon.

 Case study – Anger Management

The Referral

A 13-year-old boy has been having difficulty with dealing with his anger. His teachers describe him as an able but at times reluctant and troubled learner. Lately he has become more unmanageable, refusing to engage in learning in the classroom at times. His behaviour is better in some lessons than others. He has been 'on report' countless times, but this has had little effect. His mother is supportive and she is the lone parent. There are two other younger female siblings. He has been removed from lessons on several occasions for poor behaviour.

Action

His mother agreed, after a meeting with the Form Tutor and Head of Year, that a Learning Mentor might be helpful. The Learning Mentor wrote to the parent and followed up the letter with a phone call. The first meeting with the student was attended by the mother, who came to show her support for the process, and to encourage her son. Over a period of eight weekly meetings the Learning Mentor worked with the student to firstly build up a rapport, using listening and communication skills, and supporting the student when he had difficulties with his temper, for example by providing him with a 'Time Out' card in the short term, and developing a set of targets and an action plan that was shared (with the boy's agreement) with his mother. He was also invited to attend the half term holiday programme, thereby giving him a break from his responsibilities at home. His sisters, who attended the local primary school, were also invited to attend, providing the mother with some respite time and releasing the boy from babysitting duties. This was organised by the Learning Mentor. At the end of the eight-week period, the boy was managing his anger more effectively; he still needed help with this but the Learning Mentor had helped him develop some strategies for anger management. Additionally, by working closely with the family the Learning Mentor was able to provide help, support and an understanding of the situation, and provide tangible options, suggestions and solutions for managing the excess pressure that the young boy was feeling with regard to responsibilities in the home.

This case study demonstrates several aspects of an appropriate referral:

- A valid reason for the referral

- A person with appropriate authority made the referral

- Good communication with the family

- A structured approach to the first meeting with the student

- A negotiated plan with the student

- A period of review and reflection.

The Referral Form

The referral form should be simple to read, easy to complete and not too long. Think about the appearance of the form, consider the font type and size, spacing, use of clear space, the school logo and headings and whether there is a school or house style that you should be using. Think about whether the form should be on coloured paper for easy identification, size A5 or A4. Included here are two examples of referral forms.

The first form ('Referral to Learning Mentor') is more general and gives scope for the person making the referral to write about the student in detail. The second, 'Request for Learning Mentor Intervention', requests that the person making the referral give information about any previous strategies and interventions that have been used with the student. The aim here is to give the Learning Mentor a fuller picture of the student.

The referral form should include the obvious basic information (student name, date of birth, address and form), and information about the reason for the referral; this should meet the referral criteria, more on this below. Categories of referral might be for example anger management, attendance, punctuality, homework issues, coursework issues, family, domestic, health, medical, drugs, self harm, friendship, isolation, bullying, assertiveness and passive behaviour, and so on, depending on what is appropriate for your setting. Alternatively a space could be left for a narrative description, or perhaps even a combination of both. The criteria and definitions for referral are clear and unambiguous. The object here is to make the form fast and easy to complete, and easy to read.

Who can Refer a Student to a Learning Mentor?

A decision will need to be made about which members of staff can make referrals. This is potentially a tricky issue. You will of course want to build

REFERRAL TO LEARNING MENTOR

Student name:

Form/Class:

Home address:

Reason for referral:

Date:

Name of person referring:

Position:

Photocopiable:

The Learning Mentor Manual © Stephanie George, 2010.

REQUEST FOR LEARNING MENTOR INTERVENTION

Student name:

Form/Class:

Home address:

Please indicate here what other support or interventions have been provided for the student.

Please indicate here reasons for the request for a Learning Mentor for this student.

Date parental consent obtained:

Staff name: Staff position:

Date:

relationships quickly and effectively with teaching staff and make yourself available to help students, but you will not want to be inundated with inappropriate referrals. Suggestions of staff that could be appropriate referrers are:

- Form Tutors

- Heads of Year (or those in a similar pastoral role leading a year team)

- Heads of House

- Heads of Department

- SENCOs

- EAL Managers

- Learning Mentor Managers.

I would suggest keeping the group of those with referral rights as small as you can; this makes the whole process more manageable and also ensures that those referring are those with an overview of either a class or year group. They are likely to know what other interventions and strategies have already been implemented or attempted, and this will help avoid duplication. They are also able to look at the child as a whole and in the broadest sense, having knowledge of their learning, home circumstances and character.

Why is a Referral Process Necessary?

One of the fundamental aspects of effective provision is formalising the process of mentoring to include the referral criteria, the referral, case notes, action planning, target setting, monitoring and evaluation. It is for this reason that the referral process needs to be clear and transparent. It can be very easy to fall into the trap of seeing students on an ad hoc basis only to find that there is no formal record of ever having had the student referred. This makes it very difficult to pinpoint the effectiveness of the Learning Mentor function, and also makes for a very shaky start with the student and family. Working in this way does nothing to help make clear the status of the Learning Mentor within the organisation, and it can devalue the intervention in the eyes of students and staff. In summary, a referral process is necessary because:

- It ensure Learning Mentors are not inundated with requests to see students on an ad hoc basis

- Learning Mentors can use their time effectively, appropriately and carefully to meet the needs of their students

- It sets the standard for the Learning Mentor team, and makes its status clear to all

- It makes clear that there are sound operational procedures for the work.

The Criteria for Referral

There will be many reasons for referral to a Learning Mentor as we have already established; in order to define the criteria for a referral, consultation with the pastoral team is necessary. Normally, a discussion will take place and a decision will then be made about the criteria for referral. You will need to consider the school ethos, cohort, size and the needs of its students, and keep in mind that the role of the Learning Mentor is to help students overcome barriers to their learning. It can be helpful to begin by thinking about the students who would benefit from having a Learning Mentor, as a starting point for developing the referral criteria. The following are common reasons for needing support, which might become part of your criteria for referral:

- Students who are not meeting coursework deadlines, and are not already being mentored under other academic mentoring mechanisms

- Where it is known that family issues are affecting school work

- Where the student is having difficulty forming friendships, and is isolated

- Where there are issues of bullying, and other interventions have not resolved the situation

- Where a group of students have an unresolved issue where mediation would be helpful

- Where the student is presenting with social and emotional issues that are affecting their learning and/or the learning of their peers

- Personal issues are affecting student learning and achievement

- Where support is needed when referring the student to an external agency.

Preparing to Mentor

Once you have agreed on the criteria for referral in your school, students can then be referred and the business of mentoring can begin. When a referral has been received, an appointment needs to be made to see the student. It is vital in this meeting to lay the foundations for a good mentoring relationship between the student and the mentor. Whilst primary school students in my experience seem to be very amenable to this I have seen resistance on the part of secondary school students, and this frequently arises when there have been other unsuccessful interventions and people are becoming exasperated. There is a lot to be said for early intervention, good communication with the family and a well prepared referral form.

Building up a good relationship with the parent or carer of the student you will be mentoring is key, and included here are three examples of letters you can send home to parents when trying to set up the first meeting with them.

If you don't get a response to the letter then you'll need to follow up with a telephone call, and hopefully this will result in you setting up an appointment with the parent to discuss mentoring.

The Meeting with Parents or Carers to Discuss Mentoring

The important thing here is not to alarm the parent or carer. They are usually aware that there is an issue that needs to be worked through with the student, so a calm and sensitive approach is necessary. I would suggest covering the following in the first meeting:

- Explain the reason for the referral

- Be clear about what will happen at the mentoring appointments

- Reassure the parents about issues of confidentiality

- Explain how often their child will be mentored, when the appointments will take place, how long the appointments will be and how the school hopes the student will benefit

- Make sure parents know what records you will keep, and why they're necessary

- Invite the parents to keep in contact with you, and make arrangements for this

- Explain when you will be available, and how they can contact you

- Always keep parents informed of any developments.

Sample Letter to Parents 1

[INSERT SCHOOL LETTERHEAD]

Name of Parent/Carer

Address Line 1

Address Line 2

Address Line 3   Date

Dear [insert name of parent/carer],

Re: [insert name of student]

Your son/daughter/grandchild [insert name of student] has asked to be supported by a Learning Mentor, with regard to some difficulties they are facing in school. I would like to talk to you about this, and kindly ask that you telephone the school to make an appointment for us to discuss the matter.

I look forward to hearing from you.

Yours sincerely,

[Name of Learning Mentor or name of the Head of Department]

(This depends on your school protocol.)

 Photocopiable:
The Learning Mentor Manual © Stephanie George, 2010.

Sample Letter to Parents 2

[SCHOOL LETTERHEAD]

Name of Parent/Carer

Address Line 1

Address Line 2

Address Line 3   Date

Dear Parent/Carer,

Re: Your daughter/your son

We would like to offer the support and help of a Learning Mentor to your daughter/son [put the student's name in here]. Learning Mentors work with students to help them overcome barriers to learning. In our school, Learning Mentors run a range of workshops, sessions and programmes to help students to achieve their potential.

We would like to discuss this with you, and would ask you to telephone the school and ask for [put the name of the member of staff here] to make an appointment to discuss the matter further.

Yours faithfully,

[Name of Learning Mentor or the name of the Head of Department]

[This depends on your school protocol.]

Photocopiable:
The Learning Mentor Manual © Stephanie George, 2010.

Sample Letter to Parents 3

Dear Parent/Carer,

Re: Your daughter/your son/your grandson, etc.

We are writing to invite you to a meeting to discuss support for _____.

The school Learning Mentors assist with issues affecting learning, and we would like to discuss allocating a Learning Mentor to _____.

Please do telephone _____ to arrange a mutually convenient time to meet.

Yours faithfully,

(Name of Learning Mentor or name of the Head of Department)

(This depends on your school protocol.)

Photocopiable:
The Learning Mentor Manual © Stephanie George, 2010.

Case study – Transition

A Year 6 student had recently joined the school, and was finding the transition to her new setting difficult. The family had moved from one part of the country to another, and so the city was new as well as the school. The class teacher raised concerns about the fact that this 10-year-old girl was finding it difficult to make friends. Although the class teacher had made arrangements for the child to have a buddy, this had broken down when the buddy was away from school with chicken pox for over a week. The child did not seem to get along with the substitute buddy, and so the class teacher spoke to the Learning Mentor about the situation. The Learning Mentor was discussing the possibility of jointly running with the class teacher a Circle of Friends group, when the parents contacted the school. The parents said that the child had become withdrawn at home, was eating little and was not her usual self. The Learning Mentor made an appointment to see the parents, and explained what the school was thinking of doing. The parents were relieved that the school had in fact picked up on the unhappiness of their child and were in the process of arranging an intervention, which then took place.

In this case as the situation was moving at a brisk pace and conversations had already taken place between the class teacher and the Learning Mentor about a suitable intervention, no letter was sent to the parents. However, I would always recommend getting written consent from parents for mentoring, as usually intervention will require a student to be removed from classes and parental permission is needed for this. Sample Letter 2 invites the parent/carer into the school so that the Learning Mentor has the opportunity to discuss the referral further, answer any queries, obtain further information from the parent/carer and begin to establish a relationship with the family.

Starting to Mentor

The Learning Mentor will need a private space to meet with the student, chairs for both student and Learning Mentor, paper, pen, sometimes colouring pencils, Post-it notes or small cards and a computer for use in the mentoring session or for writing up notes afterwards. There should be a signing-in book for all students attending the Learning Mentor's base. This is useful for a quick check, should anyone wish to confirm the whereabouts of a student on a particular day.

The First Meeting with the Student

Some students may well exhibit bewilderment or bemusement at being asked to see you; some will be relieved that help is at hand and some will be worried and afraid. Students will often need reassurance. The first appointment is therefore crucial to establish the right tone, protocol and expectations for the mentoring relationship, which you want ultimately to be effective, positive and successful for the student.

The 'Step by Step Guide to the First Mentoring Appointment' guides the Learning Mentor through the initial meeting with the student.

I would suggest using this as a checklist for the appointment and it can also then be placed in the case file to show that the appropriate steps have been followed. The form helps to bring focus to the meeting and ensures some standardisation in practice for the initial meetings.

Instructions for using the Step by Step Guide to the First Mentoring Appointment follow.

1. Step 1 provides the opportunity to introduce the Learning Mentor service to the student. The student may have some preconceived ideas about mentoring, and they may be either very positive about the meeting or very resistant, even hostile. This is an opportunity to talk about the range of activities that Learning Mentors are involved in organising, such as the one-to-one meetings, the homework clubs, the holiday schemes and the peer mentoring sessions. This should help to capture the interest of the student, and it provides an overview of what mentoring can offer them. It allows for a more general start to the meeting, so that you're not immediately focusing on the student's problems. Once you've set out the opportunities mentoring can offer, you can move on to talk about the reasons for their referral.

2. Step 2 is an opportunity for the student to tell the Learning Mentor what they think the reason for referral might be. The intention is not to wrong foot the student but to slowly coax them into naming the issue for themselves, and prompt some recognition. I find that students often know exactly the reason for the referral and are only too happy to have someone to talk to about this. If the student is resistant and does not wish to speak, then gently explain what the concerns are. I have found that the reason the student gives for the referral is often quite different to the one stated on the referral form. Staff may well give you a referral that details symptoms, but the student is likely to give you the cause. This case study demonstrates what I mean.

Step by Step Guide to the First Mentoring Appointment

Step	Activity	Completed
Step 1	Introduce the Learning Mentor service	
Step 2	Explain and explore the reason for the referral	
Step 3	Discuss appointment arrangements	
Step 4	Broaden the discussion & answer questions	
Step 5	Book the next appointment	
Step 6	Closing the mentoring meeting	
Step 7	Writing up the case notes	

Case study – Year 10 student

A referral is received in the Learning Mentor office which states that the student Sheila in Year 10 is often late for lessons, with no reason given, and that she has refused to attend Coursework Club to catch up with and complete her missing assignments. Sheila owes her English and Science teachers two pieces of coursework and as well as refusing to stay behind to complete the coursework she has also refused to attend detentions. She has been rude to staff. It also appears from observation and anecdotal evidence that Sheila has a boyfriend who has been seen at the school gates. He appears to be an older boy. Shelia previously had a boyfriend in the school in Year 11 but they do not speak to each other now.

Action

On discussing the issue with the student, the Learning Mentor used open questioning, paraphrasing, summarising and close listening. Sheila explained to the Learning Mentor that although she realised that they wanted to help, she didn't want the teachers to 'know her business' and that she had 'a lot of family stuff going on'. The Learning Mentor made clear the mentoring procedures around confidentiality. Sheila eventually agreed at the end of the appointment that a Learning Mentor would be useful, and made a second appointment.

It is highly unlikely that a student will talk about what is happening in their personal lives at the first meeting. They do not know who they can trust, and they may have concerns about information about their personal lives being revealed to classroom teachers. It is absolutely vital that trust is built up gradually with students. It is important to accept what the student says at this stage, this is not the time to challenge a student; that will come later if necessary. The first appointment is all about laying the foundations for the mentoring relationship.

3. Step 3 is the time that the appointment system can be explained to the student and it gives the student an opportunity to highlight any concerns about this. This is important, particularly if mentoring is taking place during lesson time and the student is being withdrawn from class for the meetings. Many schools have a mentoring policy that permits this, as they regard mentoring interventions as valuable. Examples of good practice demonstrate that schools that are inclusive and provide strong interventions raise achievement in this way. The OfSTED (2009) report, *Twelve Outstanding Secondary Schools*, makes this point about intervention and meeting student needs.

4. Step 4 gives the student the opportunity to ask questions about the process of mentoring. If they are reluctant or slow to start, again give

them a few prompts. The purpose is to broaden the discussion, and take the spotlight off the student for a few moments. This will allow you to engage the student without talking about 'their problem'. A good tip is to tell them about another student (unnamed/one that has left), who has had Learning Mentor intervention in the past and has successfully overcome their difficulties. If the student wants to talk about the reason for their referral, or dispute it, then let them; my advice is to let the student get this out of their system. The student is then likely to be more receptive to what you have to say, if they feel that they have been listened to and that there is an understanding of their situation.

5. Step 5 is when the next appointment is booked with the student. Ask the student to get their planner out, and make the next appointment with them. Do this in an upbeat, positive and optimistic way. The message we want to convey to the student is that we expect to see them again, that we will be working with them to improve things and that this is the beginning of something positive for them.

6. Step 6 is when the mentoring appointment is brought to a close, and it is important to explicitly thank the student for attending the appointment. The student should leave with the impression and understanding that the Learning Mentor and the school value their well-being so highly that this provision has been made for them.

7. Step 7 is when a note is made for the file, either handwritten or on the computer, and a diary note is made for the next appointment.

A Model for Mentoring – the I SEE Matrix

I have developed a model for mentoring which has been tried and tested by Learning Mentors. It is called the I SEE Matrix for Learning Mentoring (see blank form given here).

I SEE is an acronym for Issue, Start, Engage and Evaluate. The matrix guides the Learning Mentor through the mentoring process when working with the student. Firstly, the Learning Mentor uses open questions, paraphrasing and summarising skills to identify the issue of concern or area to be developed with the student and this is plotted on the matrix. Secondly, the Learning Mentor explores the issue identified; this is a brainstorming session to establish how the student feels about the issue. Thirdly, the main part of mentoring takes place where there is a search to engage the student with looking at possibilities to address the issue or area for development. This Engage aspect of the I SEE Matrix is used to develop the action plan that I will be discussing in Chapter 5. Lastly, evaluation will take place and also support for the student. The evaluation aspect of the I SEE Matrix is completed at the end of the action planning implementation period. Figure 3.1 is a completed example of the I SEE Matrix.

I SEE Matrix – Example

Issue

Start

I am frequently late for school.
This is causing problems with me and teachers.
This is causing problems at home.

Why am I late for school?
I stay up late because I like to chat with friends online.
I don't know where the time goes.
No-one wakes me up.
My mum is fed up with me now – I don't like this.

Engage

Evaluate

I could get a timer, when the time is up I switch off PC.
How long does it take to get ready?
I need to get an alarm clock, ask mum by Wednesday for one.
Get help in setting the alarm.

Punctuality has improved by X%
Getting praised by teachers for getting in on time.
Phone calls to mum have stopped.
Feeling happier about school.
Need help to continue with this.

Figure 3.1 I SEE Matrix – Example

I SEE Matrix – a Model for Learning Mentoring

Start

Evaluate

Issue

Engage

Confidentiality and Learning Mentors

In Chapter 1 I talked about the Learning Mentor policy and procedures and how important it was to know about these, as well as the departmental handbooks and other school documents. One of the things that does concern students is the issue of confidentiality, and it is important. It should be made clear during the first mentoring appointment what the position is on confidentiality in any discussion between the Learning Mentor and the student. It should also be made clear what the implications are with regard to Child Protection and any discussion between the Learning Mentor and the student. Be very clear about what the school's Child Protection Policy is and how this impacts upon the Learning Mentor intervention. I think it is useful to have a written statement, particularly for secondary school children, that can be read to the student and signed by them showing that they understand what is meant by confidentiality and what the Learning Mentor will be able to keep private and what must be disclosed. In a primary setting, it is important again to explain confidentiality simply to children so that they have some understanding of what it means, so that they can feel more open about discussing things with the Learning Mentor. Policy and practice will vary from school to school, so it is essential that you and your students know what your school policy is and what this means for both of you in practice.

 Key points

1. Starting things off in the right way at the beginning of the mentoring process will give you the best chance of succeeding with the student.
2. The referral criteria for referring a student to a Learning Mentor needs to be developed in consultation with pastoral staff, and it must be a transparent process that all staff understand.
3. Working and communicating with parents and carers from the start is vitally important.

 Downloadable material

Go to www.sagepub.co.uk/george for downloadable material to this chapter.

Preparing to Mentor Checklist

Referral to Learning Mentor

Request for Learning Mentor Intervention

Sample Letter to Parents 1

Sample Letter to Parents 2

Sample Letter to Parents 3

Step by Step Guide to the First Mentoring Appointment

I SEE Matrix – a Model for Learning Mentoring

Further reading

Egan, Gerard (2001) *The Skilled Helper: A Problem-Management and Opportunity-Development Approach to Helping.* Florence, KY: Wadsworth.

Rogers, Bill (2006) *Cracking the Hard Class*, 2nd edn. London: Sage.

4

Partnerships with Internal and External Agencies

> **This chapter covers:**
> - **The role of the Learning Mentor in partnership working**
> - **The range of partnerships and stakeholders working in schools**

Working in Partnership

Partnership working is one of the key elements in fulfilling the core functional skills for Learning Mentors. The sheer range of agencies you need to deal with can be overwhelming, however – the skill is knowing how to locate the resources, information, organisations and key people when you need them, and sometimes you will need to do this very quickly indeed. The range of professionals is broad, given that Learning Mentors are to be found in a range of settings including primary, secondary or middle schools, pupil referral units, community projects and so on. The professional partners include:

- Educational Psychologists

- School Nurses

- General Practitioners

- Welfare Assistants

- Social Workers

- Police Community Support Officers

- Police Officers

- Community Wardens

- School Counsellors

- Youth Offending Team Workers

- Youth Workers

- PSHE Teachers

- Visual and Hearing Impaired Specialist Teachers

- Attendance Officers

- Education Welfare Officers (EWOs)

- Higher Level Teaching Assistants (HLTAs)

- Teaching Assistants (TAs)

- Learning Support Assistants (LSAs)

- Special Educational Needs Co-ordinators (SENCOs)

- Special Educational Needs Teachers

- Year 6 Transition Teachers

- Behaviour Advisory Teachers

- Inclusion Officers

- Parents

- Carers

- Extended Family Members

- the Senior Management Team of the organisation

- and, of course, other Learning Mentors.

In addition to this list there are a huge range of personnel that a Learning Mentor may work with in assisting young people. This is not a definitive list, but other agencies Learning Mentors are likely to come into contact with include:

- The local Connexions service

- Young Carers Support Teams

- Parent Advocacy organisations

- Sexual Health Clinics

- Anti-Bullying support networks

- Mental Health organisations

- Eating Disorder organisations

- Drugs information and awareness teams

- Alcohol information and awareness teams

- Self-Harm organisations

- Citizens Advice teams and Law Centres

- Youth Centres and the Youth Services

- City Learning Centres

- and the Local Authority for everything from housing to financial matters.

When a Learning Mentor Might Work with Other Services, Partners and Providers

The work of the Learning Mentor is led by the needs of the student, and the Learning Mentor development plan that the organisation's Learning Mentor team would have in place will make explicit the strategic direction of the team. The needs of the school and its cohort depend very much upon setting, locality, socio-economic factors, environment, culture and ethos. The demands of the school cohort will determine to some extent the range of services that the school will access and work with, in order to help students and their families to overcome barriers to learning and to support the school's ultimate aim, i.e. to ensure that students receive a broad and balanced education, avail themselves of educational opportunities such as visits, residential visits and clubs, and develop as socially and emotionally literate young people who can contribute usefully to society. However, when there are difficulties the school is well placed to help young people and their families to access a range of support services. An example of successful partnership working is detailed here in this case study.

Case study – Sean and his father

Sean is a Year 7 student who lives alone with his father and one younger sister. Sean's father has Multiple Sclerosis, a disease of the nervous system. Sean's father is sometimes unable to walk or leave the house. However, there are times when the disease abates and Sean's father is much better. Sean is responsible for taking his younger sister to school. Social services have provided a part-time carer, and there is an aunt who is sometimes able to help the family but she has her own commitments and is unable to give regular support. Sean is a hardworking, dedicated student. He is a member of the Year 7 football team. He was referred to a Learning Mentor following a meeting with Sean's aunt who attended Parents' Evening on behalf of Sean's father. Sean was very willing to talk to the Learning Mentor about his family situation, and is keen to help his father and sister. He does not talk about his mother and there is no information about her. The school is keen that Sean, who achieved Level 5 for English and Science and Level 6 for Maths at the end of Key Stage 2, achieves his full potential. The Learning Mentor made a visit to the home after discussing the situation with the school's Education Welfare Officer and it was agreed with a Senior Teacher and the Head of Year that a visit to the home would be useful. There have been concerns lately that Sean has been coming into school late. During the home visit, Sean's father is able to stand but moves very slowly and with pain. He explains that the disease affects his mobility, causing muscle spasms and weakness. He also explains that he is having some problems with his eyesight. The carer provided by social services is also at the meeting, as are the social worker and the aunt. The purpose of the meeting is to identify ways of supporting the family, and in particular to ascertain why Sean has been arriving late for school. The Learning Mentor reveals that Sean has told him that he has been taking his sister to school and then returning home to see if his father is all right and then coming to school. Following the meeting, a decision is made to contact social services and this is done in consultation with the school's senior manager responsible for Child Protection issues and also involves the Head of Year. As a result of this close communication and team working, social services provided a carer to assist the family at key points in the day, thereby relieving Sean of the responsibility that he was carrying. The Learning Mentor closely monitored the situation and continued to support Sean, inviting him to join the after school Chess Club once a week, with the agreement of the aunt and father. The aunt arranged to collect Sean's sister from school every day, so that Sean could become a permanent member of the Year 7 football team and attend fixtures. Sean's confidence continues to grow.

This case study demonstrates several key aspects of partnership working that Learning Mentors need to be aware of, in particular:

- close monitoring of student attendance, and working with the school attendance officer and form tutors

- sharing information on a need-to-know basis with Heads of Year or pastoral leaders

- consultation with senior staff

- knowledge of and due reference to Child Protection policies and procedures

- working with the school Education Welfare Officer and school social worker

- following appropriate procedures and protocols, with regard to referrals to social services

- sensitive handling of issues with students

- due regard to confidentiality policy and procedures

- knowledge of visits procedure

- sensitivity when visiting parents and families at home

- the importance of careful monitoring

- the importance of record keeping and case notes

- feedback to relevant parties.

Developing Joint Approaches with Colleagues

Building partnerships with agencies outside of the school is important, but more important are the relationships that you must develop with colleagues within the school across all departments and curriculum areas. This case study demonstrates how effective working with the Head of Year, the EWO and the Learning Mentor brought about effective change for the student and her family.

 Case study – Truanting

Stacey is a Year 11 student; there have been some problems in the home, where she lives with her mother and stepfather. Stacey and her parents have been having arguments, the catalyst for which has been their refusal to allow her to stay out late into the night, particularly on

(Continued)

(Continued)

school nights. Stacey has started to stay out late after school and refuses to tell her parents where she has been. Stacey has now started to truant from school. Stacey has been referred to the EWO and the Learning Mentor, following a meeting between the parents and Head of Year. The EWO had in fact made several visits to the home and Stacey's attendance was being monitored. At the time of the involvement of the Learning Mentor, Stacey had truanted from school for a total of three months with an unauthorised absence of over 50 days.

The Learning Mentor was able to meet Stacey, who came into school but refused to go to lessons. It was agreed that Stacey would spend the morning with the Learning Mentor to develop a programme to ease her back into school. Stacey explained that she felt she had missed so much of her schooling that there was no point in coming back to school. She also felt that she had lost many of her friends, and that her family were hostile towards her, particularly whenever the school had been in touch. The Learning Mentor sought the opinion of her teachers, who all described Stacey as a capable student when in school but lacking effort and motivation. The situation was urgent, as the deadline for examination entries was looming. In consultation with the Head of Year and Heads of Department, a decision was made that Stacey would be entered for English, Maths, Science, ICT, RE and Sociology examinations, which were subjects she really enjoyed and for which she had completed much of the coursework. Stacey agreed that she would work in the school's Learning Support Unit as part of her reintegration into school, and that the Learning Mentor would support her in completing the missing pieces of English coursework. Stacey would not be permitted to leave the school site, unlike the rest of Years 10 and 11 who were permitted to leave the school site at lunchtimes. Stacey agreed to this, saying that she did not trust herself to come back to school, and she agreed initially to have lunch with her Learning Mentor partly because she found it difficult to re-establish friendships. She slowly began to do this.

Stacey was a very angry girl, and by the time she was referred to the Learning Mentor she had a new set of friends outside school who encouraged her to drink, smoke and take drugs and she said that she saw nothing wrong with this as she was about to leave school in any event. The Learning Mentor spent some hours over the course of a period of weeks mentoring around issues of boundaries, family norms, drug abuse, alcohol abuse, mental health issues and personal safety. An important feature of the mentoring was the question of personal choice and planning for the future. The Learning Mentor was able to strike a bargain with Stacey, offering one-to-one support, attention and guidance in return for regular attendance and acting as advocate for Stacey when speaking to her parents. The relationship between Stacey and her parents was very strained. The Learning Mentor was able to arrange for the Careers Personal Advisor to see Stacey and explore post-16 options.

Encouraged and enthusiastic, Stacey asked her Learning Mentor to attend a Careers Fair with her, where Stacey started to explore courses and options around nursery nursing.

Stacey's mother however was not so enthusiastic, complaining that Stacey was uncontrollable outside school and that she was stealing money from the house. Stacey's Learning Mentor accompanied her to a Careers Day at school. Stacey was initially reluctant to attend, but with encouragement did so. With the Learning Mentor's help, Stacey applied for a college place and received a conditional offer which depended upon her achieving C grades for English, Maths and Science and D grades or above for the other subjects. Stacey eventually achieved B grades in Sociology and English, a C grade for Maths and a D grade for Science; she successfully gained a place at college to study nursery nursing.

Access to Services

Accessing services requires you to follow the procedures and protocols as set out by the setting in which you are working, and it is important that as a Learning Mentor you are aware of these. Learning Mentors will need to ensure that they receive the appropriate training and induction, together with regular updates as necessary. It is likely that there will be a nominated member of staff who is responsible for making referrals, and it is crucial that Learning Mentors know who this person is so that they can follow the appropriate procedures, or if in doubt, seek advice. In any event, such matters should always be discussed with the line manager. An activity that is helpful for focusing the mind is the one I have provided here.

 Activity

Find out what your referral procedures are for contacting external agencies. Use the form given here to help with this.

You will need to discuss this with various colleagues in your school, to ensure you have the correct information. Every Learning Mentor needs to know what to do in a situation where their work with a student leads them to feel that an outside agency needs to become involved in order to support that student effectively. It is imperative to follow the right procedures, as there may be legal implications.

Organising Information for Referral to External Agencies

The range of organisations that Learning Mentors work with is vast as we have established, and will very much depend on the needs of the student.

What are the Referral Procedures for Contacting External Agencies?	
Educational Psychologist	
Police Officers/School Support Officer	
Social Services	
Youth Offending Team	
Connexions Services	
Sexual Health Team	
Drugs Information Service	
Alcohol Information Service	
Counselling Services	
Behaviour Advisory Teachers	
Other	

 Photocopiable:

The Learning Mentor Manual © Stephanie George, 2010.

However, it is also likely that staff may ask you for information about organisations that can help with particular issues, and parents may also do the same. Therefore it is important to be able to access the information quickly, and have it organised in a methodical fashion. Something very simple but incredibly useful that I've always done is to create a list of key contacts; to do this yourself you will need:

- a PC with a word processing package

- a printer and paper

- a pack of A6 index cards

- an A6 index box card holder

- an A6 A – Z Index, to fit in the box

- scissors

- glue

- an A4 folder.

Firstly type up an electronic list of all of the organisations that the team are in regular contact with, and be sure to include the name of the organisation, the name of any particular contacts there and their telephone numbers, postal address and email addresses. Sort the list alphabetically; this will help when filing the information later on. Save the list, giving it a name and date. Print two copies of the list, file one copy in an A4 folder labelling it Learning Mentor Contacts and take the second copy and cut out each individual contact. Paste each contact onto an A6 Index card, one per card. File the cards alphabetically, and keep the index box in a convenient place on your desk (but keep the A4 folder on a shelf). This way, you will always have key contacts immediately to hand, and at the beginning of each academic year you can review and update this list.

Raising the Profile of the Learning Mentor with Families

Good communication with families is vital, and the practical aspects of this are important. Learning Mentors can begin developing a good working relationship with parents before there are any concerns. A strong visible presence at open evenings, parents' evenings and similar school events can be established throughout the school year. A good starting place is the school open evenings, which usually occur in the autumn term. This is an opportunity to show the breadth of work that the Learning Mentor team are involved with. I have mapped out some suggestions in Figure 4.1.

DISPLAY MATERIALS	
CREATING EVIDENCE OF LEARNING MENTOR INTERVENTION	
Displays of student work	Copies of notes from brainstorming sessions, e.g. Conflict Mediation or Anger Management sessions (this will need to be displayed in such a way as to avoid revealing student identity).
Written feedback	Feedback from staff on improvements they have seen in students. Feedback from students on their own progress.
Publicity about Learning Mentors	Create a leaflet explaining all about the work of the Learning Mentors. This could be an annual job, prepared in the summer term. Do not print it until the first week of the new autumn term, just in case there are any last minute staff changes.
Display books produced from work with students	Throughout the year create large A3 sized display books, the ones with transparent sleeves, and enlarge work that students have completed and add these to the book. These books can be themed, e.g. Holiday Scheme, Homework Club, Peer Mediation.
Photographs	Create displays showing students involved in activities organised by Learning Mentors, e.g. holiday schemes, clubs and workshops. Make sure that there is parental consent for any photographs taken and displayed in the school in this way.

Figure 4.1   Display Ideas

Once a display is created, if laminated it can be carefully taken down, placed in a box, labelled and used again at the next event. Keep the box in an easily accessible place and any interesting pieces of work can be photo-copied, mounted, laminated and added to the box ready for the next event. This way, the display always looks fresh as items are being added to the resource throughout the year. I would urge you to use the opportunities that twilight and evening events provide for meeting parents, they are invaluable.

Think about writing a piece for the parents' newsletter or bulletin about the work of the Learning Mentors. Aim to have a piece in once a term. A regular brief reminder of the work of the Learning Mentors can be supplemented by larger, celebratory pieces with photographs.

Working with Governors

The governing body are the school's strategic partners and critical friends. The governing body is typically made up of community governors, the local authority or administrative county governors, staff governors and parent governors. As a body they have an interest in the strategic direction of the school, the school's policies, school profile, school development plan and the school's achievements. Governors therefore have an interest in the work of Learning Mentors as agents for overcoming barriers to learning. Learning Mentors and their teams should take opportunities to share their work with the governing body, and below are a number of ways that this can be done.

1. Consider contributing to the Headteacher's report to the governing body. There may already be opportunities for this, but if not discuss with your line manager. Writing a brief article once or twice a year will raise the profile of the work of Learning Mentors. Think about using some of the evaluations from students, and include feedback from students if appropriate. My suggestions for contributions to the report for the governing body include information about group work and its effectiveness, statistics giving evidence of the number of students seen in a given term, or participating in a special event, e.g. Christmas play, or sporting or musical events.

2. Consider inviting a governor to visit the Learning Mentor base for part of a working day to see mentoring in action, and try to choose a day when there is an event going on, e.g. a day when Learning Mentors are running a special session on something like peer mentor training, or an anti-bullying workshop.

3. Consider inviting governors to an event where students who have been mentored are taking part, particularly where a student has overcome difficulties. This is a good opportunity to share success, and this can, of course, also be shared with parents.

Thinking prompt:

- In what ways do you as a Learning Mentor currently keep governors informed about your work?

- Is there a governor that has an interest in the work of a Learning Mentor?

- Is there a staff governor that could become involved?

> ## O══ Key points
> 1. Working in partnerships with internal and external partners is an essential part of your role.
> 2. It is essential to develop an awareness of the range of external agencies that Learning Mentors work with to support students, and to be aware of how and when to access them.
> 3. Raising the profile of Learning Mentors with governors can reap real benefits.

Downloadable material

Go to www.sagepub.co.uk/george for downloadable material to this chapter.

What are the Referral Procedures for Contacting External Agencies?

Further reading

The Children's Workforce Development Council, for an understanding of how different agencies can work together, at: www.cwdcouncil.org.uk

5

Accountability and Monitoring

> **This chapter covers:**
> - **Assessment and accountability for Learning Mentors**
> - **Issues around monitoring**
> - **Evaluation methods**

Assessment

Assessment is an important part of the work of a Learning Mentor. It is important for several reasons, including:

- to measure the progress of the student

- enabling the student to be aware of their own progress

- to provide evidence of the impact of Learning Mentor intervention

- to demonstrate how the Learning Mentor intervention is making a contribution to moving students on, in terms of whole school achievement

- to provide information for student reports to parents

- to provide data for internal systems

- to provide data for external reporting

- to provide information and data to governors

- to provide evidence of impact at a strategic level

- for purposes of transparency and accountability.

A suggested definition of assessment offered by Capel et al. (2001: 287) is that 'assessment covers all those activities that are undertaken ... to measure the effectiveness of teaching and learning'. This definition is useful as it can be applied to the mentoring context. First and foremost, Learning Mentors are concerned in removing barriers to learning. Therefore it is vital that Learning Mentors are able to demonstrate whether mentoring has made a difference to the student's life, progress and achievement.

Methods of Assessment

Assessment can be broadly divided into formative or summative. Formative assessment opportunities occur throughout the teaching and learning phase, and summative assessment usually occurs at the end of a teaching and learning phase, e.g. the SATs or GCSE examinations. Assessment provides the Learning Mentor with knowledge and information about the student, so that the mentor can assist the student with making progress. Assessments within mentoring occur at the beginning of mentoring in terms of providing baseline data and information, throughout the mentoring intervention and again at the end of mentoring. We can see that mentoring embraces both formative and summative assessment methods. Formative assessment can help to shape the course and method of mentoring intervention. A decision may be made following assessment that the student is a candidate for group work intervention, or that one-to-one mentoring is more appropriate. A list of assessment methods is provided here for your reference in Figure 5.1.

Assessment within Learning Mentoring

It is vital that the student does not feel that mentoring is another test or exam that they have to 'pass'. It should be made clear to the student that any assessment carried out within the context of Learning Mentoring is essential to monitor their progress, help them to plot their own journey and assist them in providing evidence and demonstrating their own achievements first and foremost.

Assessment helps the Learning Mentor and the student to establish a baseline, a starting point from which to measure progress. The outcome can be surprising, enlightening or even confirm a belief, opinion or understanding. Assessment methods that Learning Mentors can use are:

- Questioning (which can involve challenging student perceptions)

- Discussing 'What if?' scenarios with the student

- Student self-assessment

- Target setting

Methods of assessment, monitoring and evaluation and ways of recording interventions

1 Baseline Assessments

2 Initial Meeting

3 Attendance Registers

4 Databases

5 Mark Books

6 Written Evaluations

7 Oral Evaluations

8 Targets

9 Observations

10 Action Plans

11 Reports

12 Student Records

13 Learning Mentor Meetings

14 One-to-One Interviews

15 Year Team Meetings

16 Comments Books

17 Staff Questionnaire

18 Parental Questionnaire

19 Focus Groups

20 Student Questionnaire

Figure 5.1 Methods of Assessment

- Action planning

- Observation

- Action planning reviews.

Questioning

Questioning is an integral part of mentoring, and allows the mentor to explore and clarify areas of uncertainty as well as giving the student a chance to state their point of view. Using open questions, Learning Mentors can give the student room to explore issues freely. In the assessment stage of mentoring, questions that begin with the word 'why?' are used with caution, as they tend at the early stages of mentoring to lead to a student becoming defensive in their responses which is not desirable.

Questions such as the ones I have listed below can help with early exploratory formative assessment work:

1. Tell me some more about that?

2. Could you explain that to me?

3. That is interesting; in what ways could that have been done differently?

4. Tell me how you came to make that decision?

5. Please can you describe that for me?

Challenging Students' Perceptions

Another key aspect of mentoring is to challenge students' perceptions. It is not unusual to hear a student say in a mentoring appointment, 'I can't do that because ...'. What they are doing is limiting their own progress through thought. A major part of mentoring is challenging students' perceptions and exploring the reasons why something might be possible as opposed to why it is not possible, using the negative perception that the student has brought to the mentoring session and looking at positive possibilities with the student.

Developing 'What if?' Scenarios with the Student

The 'what if?' scenario is a powerful formative assessment tool to use with a student. I have provided a group of four 'What if?' cards for use in a mentoring session. When working with the student, the Learning Mentor can use the cards in the context of challenging perceptions and developing the 'What if?' scenario with the student.

The sample dialogue below illustrates how to use the cards:

Student: There's no point going to college next year, I know I won't get the grades I need.
Mentor: (turns the 'what if' card face up)
     What if ... you did get the grades that you need?
Student: I might be able to go to the college then.
Mentor: What if ... you went to college?
Student: I might be able to take A Levels.
Mentor: What if you were able to take A levels?

The purpose is to use the 'What if ...' and phrasing at the beginning of the response to the student and to use the student's own responses to

'What if?' Mentoring Cards

What if

What if

What if

What if

Photocopiable:
The Learning Mentor Manual © Stephanie George, 2010.

finish the 'What if ..' sentence. The cards help to focus the student on the possibilities.

Student Self-Assessment

There are several methods of student self-assessment the Learning Mentor could use:

- student self-assessment questionnaire

- a self-rating form

- Strength and Difficulties Questionnaire (Goodman, 1999)

- PASS – Pupil Attitude to Self and School*

- SNAP-B – Special Needs Assessment Programme – Behaviour*

- SNAP-Ld – Special Needs Assessment Programme – Learning Difficulties*

All of the above can be used for assessment and diagnostic purposes. One of the key things here is to obtain the student's opinion on their own progress, and how they feel about where they are at the start of mentoring before going ahead. For this purpose I think a simple self-assessment questionnaire developed for the students in your particular organisation or setting is vital. The 'Student Self-Assessment Form' given here provides an example that can be adapted.

In this example I have provided an open question for the student to talk a little about themselves, as I think this is an opportunity for them to express themselves that you can later refer to, particularly when you might need to revisit the purpose of the mentoring or provide motivation for the student.

Drafting your Assessment Tool

There is a lot to think about when designing and developing a student self-assessment tool, and you may have to design a couple for different purposes. Learning Mentoring has at its heart the requirement and desire to really address the needs of the student, and here is one area where personalisation is paramount, as the needs of the students are so diverse. Here is a list of factors to consider when designing a self-assessment tool for your setting.

- attendance, punctuality and truancy

- confidence as a learner

---

*These assessment methods are available through the British Education and Training Technology Event (www.Bettshow.com).

STUDENT SELF-ASSESSMENT FORM

Student Name:

Instructions: Please give yourself a rating for each of the categories below, using the following scale: Scale 1 for Unsatisfactory and 5 for Excellent. Circle the appropriate number.

1. I would describe my attendance as:

1	2	3	4	5

2. I would describe my punctuality as:

1	2	3	4	5

3. I would describe my relationships with other students at school as:

1	2	3	4	5

4. I would describe my relationships with teachers as:

1	2	3	4	5

5. I would describe my approach to learning as:

1	2	3	4	5

6. Tell us a little bit about yourself and school:

Your Signature...Today's Date................

Photocopiable:

The Learning Mentor Manual © Stephanie George, 2010.

- attitude to school and to teachers

- approach to (and attitude towards) learning

- enjoyment of learning

- friendship issues

- willingness or refusal to participate

- co-operative / non-co-operative

- motivation and effort

- achievement and prior attainment

- SEN information

- EAL information

- gifted and talented information

- exclusion records (detention records or sanctions or reports)

- health or medical needs

- membership of extra curricular groups

- special aptitudes, e.g. PE, sports, dance, art, etc.

- parental support

- out of school achievements, e.g. Duke of Edinburgh Award.

Action Planning and Target Setting

Best practice in Learning Mentoring requires target setting and action planning with the student, as the student needs to plan how they will make progress and what they need to do to get there. The action plan should have SMART features, i.e. it should be Specific, Measurable, Achievable, Realistic, and Time focused. The 'Target Setting and Action Plan' form given here is a sample that can be used for mentoring.

Observation of the Student

Objective observation of the student in a range of settings in the school is a useful assessment tool. Observation can focus upon such matters as the student's

Target Setting and Action Plan

Date:

Student Name:

Class/Form:

What do I want to achieve? (TARGET)	When do I want to achieve it?	How will I achieve my goal?	Who will help me with this?	How will I know I have achieved my goal? (EVIDENCE)

interaction with others, the student at play, the student in unsupervised settings, the student with different teachers and members of staff, the student at lunchtimes and so on. In this way useful information can be gleaned across a range of observational settings, but bear in mind the student's behaviour may change if they are aware that they are being observed.

Record Keeping

Record keeping is clearly vital, so that evidence can be provided of the Learning Mentor's work. A record should be kept of each mentoring appointment, with the date, time and brief notes of what was discussed with the student. Given here is a sample 'Learning Mentor Tracking Sheet', which you can use for recording interventions. This document is used to record Learning Mentor sessions with the student.

The student's name and class or form is recorded at the top of the form. The resource provides room for six appointments. The rationale behind this is that there may be opportunities for six weekly appointments either:

- within a traditional half-term period, which consist of six to eight weeks per half term

- within the new six term year, which consists of approximately six to seven weeks each term.

There is a column provided for the date of the mentoring appointment and a column for the time of the mentoring appointment. The column provided for the time of the appointment is given for additional tracking purposes. Information in this column helps the Learning Mentor to avoid withdrawing the student from lessons at the same time each week. The last column is entitled 'Session Content and Goals Agreed for this Session', here the Learning Mentor will record a summary of the mentoring appointment and any action points, which can then be referred to at the next appointment and provides information for parents, carers or pastoral leaders.

Initial assessments with the student to identify the student's particular needs are key, and these must be recorded. Keep your records clear and concise, and make sure you have an electronic and hard copy wherever possible. Ensure your records are easily accessible, as Learning Mentors are often called upon to produce records and evidence of interventions quickly. It is not uncommon for a Learning Mentor to be called upon to provide a record of meetings and actions in an emergency. Do not be caught off guard. Get into the habit of recording all interventions as soon as you can, and always before you leave school each day. Here are a few guidelines on record keeping:

LEARNING MENTOR TRACKING SHEET

Student Name:			Class/Form:

Session No.	Time of Appointment	Date of Mentoring Appointment	Session Content and Goals Agreed for this Session
1.			
2.			
3.			
4.			
5.			
6.			

Photocopiable:
The Learning Mentor Manual © Stephanie George, 2010.

- Use your professional judgement about what needs to be recorded.

- Be respectful of your student's dignity.

- Be mindful of your school's Child Protection policy at all times.

- Involve the student in the review and monitoring of the planned programme and action plan.

- Record progress and achievements.

- Inform parents, teachers and colleagues of student achievements. This really does help to motivate and encourage a student, particularly where opportunities for praise have hitherto been limited.

- Keep evidence of achievements, e.g. notes from other teachers, assessment papers, photographs that show involvement in a particular project, leaflets or programmes that name the student as having contributed to an aspect of school life.

Monitoring

Monitoring essentially involves keeping an eye on things, and ensuring that what should be happening is happening. However, monitoring should be flexible enough to allow for change. If the agreed plan is not working for the student, then it should be reviewed with the student and altered accordingly. Monitoring helps the Learning Mentor and student to see where they are going, how far they have to go and whether in fact they are on the right road. Monitoring allows for a change of plan without anxiety, and for a look back at the road travelled.

It allows the student to see evidence of their progress and to reflect upon positive changes and improvements. Equally, monitoring can reveal where a change of direction is needed in order to best meet the needs of the student. Monitoring will involve meetings with the student where feedback is given. Feedback is very important for the student, and Black et al. suggest that 'feedback which focuses on what needs to be done can encourage all to believe that they can improve. Such feedback can enhance learning' (Black et al., 2003: 46). In terms of monitoring the learning mentor intervention, it is crucial that what has been discussed at meetings is recorded in a factual way.

Evaluation

A key task at the end of a period of mentoring intervention is to evaluate the impact that Learning Mentoring has had upon the student. There are several ways to do this; one of the ways of evaluating impact is to carry out a formal but simple evaluation in written form. The 'Learning Mentor Student Evaluation' form given here is a useful form to use that is student friendly. As you can see the student is asked to give their opinion about a range of statements that relate to their relationships in school, their independence as learners, working with others and attendance and punctuality, amongst other aspects. The student completes the form and the Learning Mentor then totals up the ratings to quantify the responses.

Other methods of evaluation include individual interviews with students and discussing with them the effectiveness of the mentoring. Group interview sessions can work, where groups of students are able to evaluate the effectiveness of a particular session, unit of work or group that the Learning Mentor has developed or delivered; this is a useful method of evaluation. Keeping a comments book that students are able to access and where they can write down their own comments on the session is another way if your setting feels it is appropriate. Another method is to have postcards or slips of paper and a posting box at the entrance of the Learning Mentor base, and students are then able to give anonymous feedback if they wish to by writing down their comments and posting them into the box. It is helpful to students to reflect upon the process of working with a Learning Mentor, and crucial for the development of practice for the Learning Mentor to evaluate their work with the student.

As well as students evaluating the experience of having a Learning Mentor, it is useful for the school to reflect on what parents think about the intervention and also what other school staff have to say.

Parents Evaluating the Learning Mentor Intervention

We involve parents fairly early on when thinking about involving a Learning Mentor to help the student overcome barriers to learning. In order to complete the process and close the circle so to speak, we need to think about asking parents if they feel their children have benefited from having a Learning Mentor. Below is a list of questions that I think are suitable to ask parents.

- Has the child benefited from having a Learning Mentor?

- Has the child's interaction with other students improved?

- Has the child's relationships with teachers and other adults in the school improved?

- Has the child been helped to meet their coursework deadlines?

LEARNING MENTOR STUDENT EVALUATION FORM

We would like to find out how having a Learning Mentor has helped you. Please read each question and circle the answer which best describes your thoughts and opinions.

Has having a Learning Mentor helped you with the following:	Choose ONE answer and circle it			
Improved the way that I communicate with others?	Definitely	A little	Unsure	No
Helped me to improve my relationship with teachers?	Definitely	A little	Unsure	No
Helped me to improve my relationship with other pupils?	Definitely	A little	Unsure	No
Helped me to work more independently?	Definitely	A little	Unsure	No
Helped me to work co-operatively with other people in a team?	Definitely	A little	Unsure	No
Helped me to explain my point of view more clearly?	Definitely	A little	Unsure	No
Helped me to listen more carefully to other people's point of view?	Definitely	A little	Unsure	No
Helped me to manage my feelings?	Definitely	A little	Unsure	No
Helped me to feel more confident about myself?	Definitely	A little	Unsure	No
Helped me with my punctuality and timekeeping?	Definitely	A little	Unsure	No
Helped me to focus on my studies?	Definitely	A little	Unsure	No
Helped me to focus on my long-term ambitions?	Definitely	A little	Unsure	No

Do you have any comments to make? (Write them down below)

Thank you for completing this form.

Photocopiable:

The Learning Mentor Manual © Stephanie George, 2010.

- Has the child developed a more positive approach to homework?

- Has the child improved their organisational skills?

- Has the child improved their social skills?

- Have you been kept fully informed by the Learning Mentor of the process?

- Would you have liked more information about the Learning Mentor process?

- Were you given opportunities to meet with your child's Learning Mentor to discuss their progress?

- Do you have any suggestions for ways we could improve the process?

- Do you have any other comments?

School Staff Evaluating the Learning Mentor Intervention

I think that it is very important to take account of and review the thoughts of staff with regard to Learning Mentoring. The relationship between other staff in the school and the Learning Mentor needs to be mutually supportive if the aim of assisting, guiding and supporting students is to be maximised. You might want to consider devising a questionnaire, speaking with staff, or convening a focus group or special meeting to ascertain colleagues' views on the process. I have provided some potential questions to ask staff.

- Do you think Learning Mentors are having a positive effect upon the students in the school?

- Do you know know how to make a referral to a Learning Mentor?

- Do you feel staff are kept informed of the nature of the Learning Mentor work with students?

- Do you feel that students are making good use of the Learning Mentor service?

- Do students know how to make an appointment to see a Learning Mentor?

- Do staff know the range of support offered by the Learning Mentor?

- Do you feel that you can get information, support and guidance from the Learning Mentor with regard to students in your classes?

- Do you have any other comments?

Conclusion

There are so many ways of conducting evaluations and assessments, and the monitoring tools go hand in hand with these. I have provided a summary of the ones I have used in my mentoring earlier in this chapter (see Figure 5.1). I consider the key factors in effective assessment, monitoring and evaluation to be:

- a clear starting point for the student

- a focus for the discussion

- a baseline from which to work

- clear goal setting and action planning with the student

- an opportunity for reflection

- opportunities to improve the student's learning

- a mechanism for systematically recording the student's progress

- evidence of improvement

- early identification of specific needs, e.g. SEN, EAL and able students.

Monitoring provides opportunities for early identification of problems or issues in the student's life, and changes can then be made to the programme of mentoring to better meet the student's needs. There is transparency in terms of the student's progress, and interim reporting is possible.

Finally, evaluation provides opportunities to celebrate student progress, to review, develop and adapt interventions, to plan effectively for further interventions, to report to governors and stakeholders and for the Learning Mentor to review the impact of the intervention.

> **Key points**
> 1. Monitoring, assessing and evaluating the Learning Mentor intervention and how this can impact positively on the student is a vital part of your role.
> 2. Consider ways of evaluating the impact of mentoring in your school by looking at the range of opportunities for evaluation.
> 3. Begin to explore resources for developing baseline assessment of students, and consider the range of assessment tools you can use with the students in your setting.

Downloadable material

Go to www.sagepub.co.uk/george for downloadable material to this chapter.

'What if?' Mentoring cards

Student Self-Assessment Form

Target Setting and Action Plan

Learning Mentor Tracking Sheet

Learning Mentor Student Evaluation Form

Further reading

Black, P. and William, D. (1998) *Inside the Black Box*. London: King's College.

Go to the DCSF website at: www.standards.dcsf.gov.uk

6

Keeping it Going

This chapter covers:

- **Ways to ensure that Learning Mentor practice is embedded within the school**
- **Ideas to ensure that students can access Learning Mentor provision within the school**
- **Ideas for Learning Mentors to facilitate their own Continuing Professional Development**

Embedding Learning Mentor Practice in your School

This, I think, is a key concern and it is something you need to constantly bear in mind, particularly when looking at self-evaluation. There are a number of ways of ensuring that the work of the Learning Mentor becomes embedded in the school. Keeping a high profile for the Learning Mentor provision is one of the strategies that can be used, and by that I mean using opportunities to keep the work of the Mentor at the forefront of the minds of students and staff. On a daily basis this can be done by ensuring that visible representation of the work of the Learning Mentor is apparent. Take a walk along the corridors of your school and ask yourself if there are any representations of the work of the Learning Mentor in the school? Here are some of the areas that I think you should look at for places to display examples:

- a classroom in each department

- a form room in each year group

- the school Learning Resource Centre or Library

- the ICT suite

- on information or plasma screens

- the Main Hall

- a Head of Year's office

- the main corridors and walkways

- dining areas

- the playground and outdoor spaces

- the school reception areas.

This is an interesting and illuminating activity, please try it and see what you find. I would also suggest conducting a similar survey but this time examining school documents. Ask yourself a similar question, i.e. can readers see any reference to the work of the Learning Mentor in key school documents? I would suggest that the route for this document review should be as follows:

- Anti-Bullying Policy

- Behaviour Policy

- School Development Plan

- School Newsletter

- School Bulletins

- Reports to Parents

- Reports to Governors

- Headteacher Reports

Hopefully it will be discovered that the work of the Learning Mentor is mentioned or referred to in these documents, and in particular that there are interesting articles and reports to parents and governors which cover the broad range of activities provided by Learning Mentors.

A View from the Outside

It certainly is worth putting yourself in the place of a visitor; what can be seen when looking from the outside? Support for students should be apparent, students should be able to self-refer if they wish with ease; Learning Mentors should be approachable and welcoming and their base should be located in a place that can be easily accessed. Information about how to access the service should be freely available to students.

The Student View

Do you know what a Learning Mentor does? I actually asked a student this question some years ago. The following case study demonstrates one of the ways in which the role of the Learning Mentor can be misinterpreted.

 Case study – Florence

Florence was asked to see a Learning Mentor by her Head of House. Florence was a Year 10 student, popular in school but not so popular at home. Her mother made the request that Florence be allocated a Learning Mentor due to her lack of focus in the previous three months. Florence achieved good SATs results and was expected to achieve good GCSEs and she was certainly on target to easily achieve 5 A–C Grades. Florence did not attend the first appointment, so the Learning Mentor sent another message to her Form Tutor asking Florence to attend a subsequent appointment. Florence made it clear to her Form Tutor that she would not attend, as she did not see any reason to. The Learning Mentor made arrangements to meet Florence during lesson time to find out what the issue was. Florence was rude and off-hand with the Learning Mentor, saying 'I don't have any problems, and anyway I am an A–C student so go away. I know that you see people with problems … I am not going to tell you anything.' This sort of response is not unheard of. Florence perceived the Learning Mentors as dealing with students who needed academic help, and help with what she termed 'problems'. Learning Mentors need to ensure that their activities are balanced, and that they reach the breadth of students within the student body, so that they do not become a marginalised service.

Continuing Professional Development

There are countless opportunities for Learning Mentors to develop their own professional practice. It does seem to be the case with Learning Mentors that the more accomplished they become, particularly with their work with the more challenging students, the less keen schools are to release them for external CPD. However, CPD is crucial. The range of opportunities that exist include:

- external courses

- coaching

- mentoring

- reviewing texts, journals and literature

- attending network forums

- collaborating with other Learning Mentors

- sharing expertise with other schools and organisations

- shadowing

- further academic study

- whole school in-service training, with an external trainer brought in

- departmental in-service training with external trainer brought in

- observation and feedback from colleagues.

Leave No Stone Unturned

A useful way to ensure that you have covered as many aspects of the school as possible in terms of embedding practice and raising awareness is to look through the 'Learning Mentor Awareness' form given here. This provides you with an overview of a range of opportunities for raising awareness across the school.

Use Figure 6.1 'Promoting and Embedding Learning Mentor Provision' to personalise and map the opportunities for raising awareness in your own setting.

Another thing that I like to do is to ask a teacher what they know about the Learning Mentor team, a bit like a Q&A session but very informal. What we can glean from these informal conversations is so useful, because the responses are usually frank and true. Ask students too, it is such a valuable exercise when they feel there is no pressure to 'get it right'. Talk to other Learning Mentors about how they keep the service in the minds of staff, parents and students, and share ideas and adapt them for your setting.

Use the 'Personalised Map of Opportunities to Promote and Embed Learning Mentor Provision' to help you highlight all the ways you can promote the service you offer.

			Yes	No
1.	Do teachers know how to refer a student to a Learning Mentor?			
2.	Are the referral procedures readily available to all staff?			
3.	Is there a Learning Mentor policy and where can it be found?			
4.	Do students know how to contact a Learning Mentor?			
5.	Are students aware of the ways in which a Learning Mentor may be able to assist them?			
6.	Are parents well informed about the role of the Learning Mentor within your school?			
7.	Are governors well informed about the role of the Learning Mentor within school?			
8.	Are other non-teaching staff well informed about the role of the Learning Mentor?			

INSTRUCTIONS

- Count up how many ticks in the No column
- Count up how many ticks in the Yes column

This will now give an overview of awareness, which can be used to help plan what areas need to be developed.

PROMOTING and EMBEDDING LEARNING MENTOR PROVISION

Open Evenings		Parents' Evenings	Residentials
Newsletters		Presentations to Governing Body	Reports to Governors
Staff Meetings		Playground/Break Duties	Assemblies
Borough Network Meetings/Forums		Local and National Press	Professional Development
Notice Boards		Website/Page Presence	Departmental Leaflets
School Trips		Visits	Departmental Display Books
Comment Books		Evaluations and Feedback	Staff Handbook Information
School Prospectus		Celebratory Events	Leading Special Events

Figure 6.1 Promoting and Embedding Learning Mentor Provision

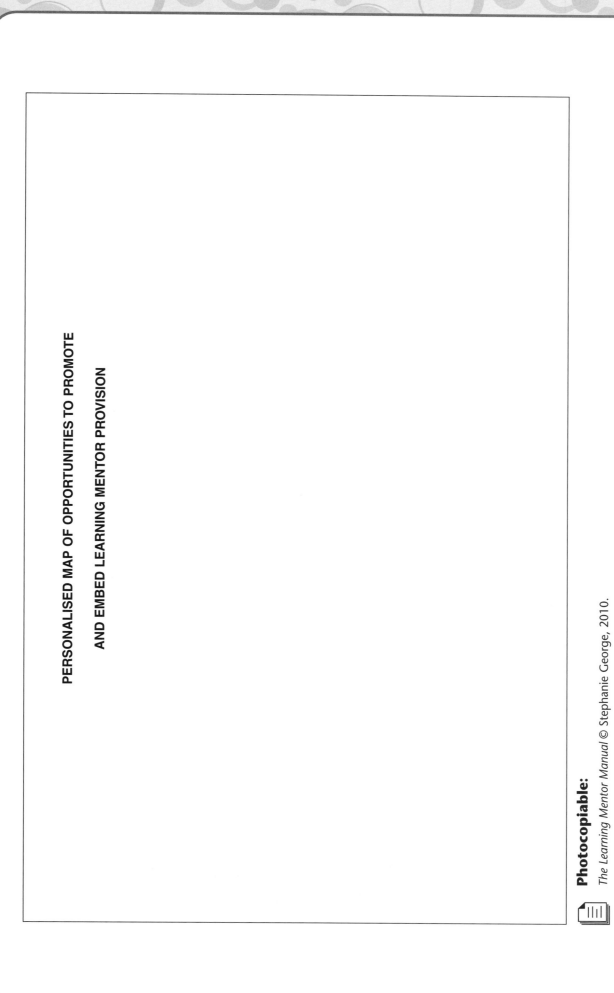

PERSONALISED MAP OF OPPORTUNITIES TO PROMOTE

AND EMBED LEARNING MENTOR PROVISION

Celebrating Uniqueness

Finally, consider whether there is anything that is particularly special about the work of the Learning Mentor team in the school. Are there special talents amongst the team? Have the team been involved in any high profile projects? I would like to share with you this example.

 Case study – the salon

I was involved in working with a group of students who were often late to lessons, as they would spend their lunchtimes involved in 'beauty activities'. What I mean by this is they would be combing each other's hair and applying henna mendhi on their hands. When they arrived in lessons they would invariably say to the teacher that they had been busy at lunchtime and had to finish off their hair styles, or that the mendhi was drying on their hands, and that they were not able to write as a consequence. This often led to an escalation, with the student vociferously making their point and the teacher just wanting to get on with teaching the lesson. As a result the Headteacher at the time 'banned' hair dressing and beauty activities. I worked with the students to develop a solution and bid for some funding to open a school salon. The salon was a huge success, with schools visiting from across London. The important thing about this is that the students were publicly acknowledged for their efforts, and in fact had the opportunity to meet the then Schools Minister David Miliband. This was a wonderful opportunity for the students to demonstrate skills of self-management, independence, teamwork and maturity. One of the benefits was how well the students developed their negotiation skills and diplomacy, and how these skills transferred to the classroom. The students also went on to be featured in the national press.

Be sure to celebrate the successes of students. Learning Mentors work with students to overcome barriers to learning, and when this happens there is cause for celebration. This is after all what the purpose of mentoring is – to ensure that students reach their full potential and achieve all they are capable of.

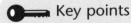 Key points
- Spend some time raising awareness of the work of the Learning Mentor within your school.
- Look for ways in which the Learning Mentor can find opportunities to share good practice and successful ideas to improve Learning Mentor provision.
- Spend some time developing a range of publicity materials that can be displayed throughout the school.

Downloadable material

Go to www.sagepub.co.uk/george for downloadable material to this chapter.

Learning Mentor Awareness

Personalised Map of Opportunities to Promote and Embed Learning Mentor Provision

Further reading 📖

Go to the website of the mentoring and befriending organisation at: www.mandbf.org.uk

Useful Websites

www.cwdcouncil.org.uk (Children's Workforce Development Council)

www.cwdcouncil.org.uk/learning-mentors

www.mandbf.org.uk (Mentoring and Befriending Foundation)

www.standards.dcsf.gov.uk (Department for Children, Schools and Families, Standards Site)

Bibliography

Bishop, S. (2008) *Running a Nurture Group*. London: Sage Publications.

Black, P. and William, D. (1998) *Inside the Black Box*. London: King's College.

Black, Paul, Harrison, Chris, Lee, Claire, Marshall, Bethan and William, Dylan (2003) *Assessment for Learning: Putting it into Practice*. Maidenhead: Open University Press.

Buzan, T. (1984) *Use your Memory*. London: BBC Books.

Canter, L. and Canter, M. (1977) *Assertive Discipline*. Los Angeles: Lee Canter Associates.

Capel, Susan, Leask, Marilyn and Turner, Tony (2001) *Learning to Teach in the Secondary School: A Companion to School Experience*, 3rd revised edn. London: Routledge Falmer.

Clutterbuck, David (1999) *Everyone Needs a Mentor*, 2nd edn. London: Chartered Institute of Personnel and Development.

Colley, Helen (1999) 'The Present According to a Past we Never Had', *Careers Guidance Today*, 7(44): 35–9.

Colley, Helen (2003) *Mentoring for Social Inclusion*. London: Routledge.

Department for Education and Employment (DfEE) (1999) *Excellence in Cities*. London: DfEE Publications.

Department for Education and Employment (DfEE) (1999) *Social Inclusion: Pupil Support*, Circular 11/99. London: DfEE Publications.

Department for Education and Skills (DfES) (2001) *Learning Mentors: A Good Practice Guide*. London: DfES Publications.

Department for Education and Skills (DfES) (2004) *Every Child Matters: Change for Children*. London: DfES Publications.

Egan, Gerard (2001) *The Skilled Helper: A Problem-Management and Opportunity-Development Approach to Helping*. Florence, KY: Wadsworth.

Goodman, R. (1999) *Strength and Difficulties Questionnaire*. www.sdqinfo.com

OfSTED (2003) *Excellence in Cities and Education Action Zones: Management and Impact*. Manchester: OfSTED.

OfSTED (2009) *Twelve Outstanding Secondary Schools: Excelling Against the Odds*. Manchester: OfSTED.

Rogers, Bill (2006) *Cracking the Hard Class*, 2nd edn. London: Paul Chapman Educational Publishing.

Zunker, Vernon G. (2005) *Career Counseling: A Holistic Approach*. Florence, KY: Brooks Cole.

Index

Note: the letter 'f' after a page number refers to a figure; the letter 's' refers to a photocopiable sheet.

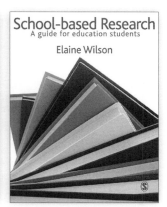

Exciting Education Texts from SAGE

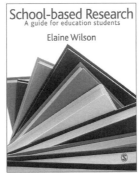

978-1-4129-4850-0

978-1-4129-4818-0

978-1-84787-917-2

978-1-84787-018-6

978-1-84787-943-1

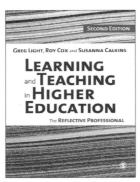

978-1-84860-008-9

978-1-84787-362-0

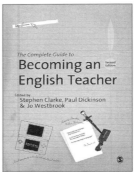

978-1-84787-289-0

978-1-84920-076-9

Find out more about these titles and our wide range of books for
education students and practitioners at **www.sagepub.co.uk/education**